A Glamorously Unglamorous Life

JULIA ALBAIN

Distributed by Argo Navis Author Services

To my parents, brother, and sister,
who believe in me so much that I'm forced
to believe in myself as well.

To my beautiful friend family for
making me laugh until it hurts, teasing me
to keep me humble, and giving me back
a true sense of purpose.

To the New Yorkers who saw me
at my worst and love me anyway.

FOREWORD:
A YEAR LATER

It's a strange feeling to dive back into a project from a year ago, a project which was a reflection on a year prior to that. It's a strange thing to admit to yourself that even when you have new answers, they aren't all the answers, and one day you'll probably find that even your answers aren't that relevant anymore. It's a strange thing to realize that as time passes a lot changes and, at the same time, nothing changes. Two years removed from the experiences this book details, and one year removed from writing it, I feel no less questioning than any time before. As I've learned new answers, they've only been partnered with new questions. So the journey now is about finding peace in the questions.

As I write this, and as I put the finishing edits into place (cursing past Julia for such grammatical laziness) I am sitting in a coffee shop listening to two thirteen-year-old girls at the table next to me recount all the things they absolutely know about what life is and what people are and what their future holds. I want to walk over and hug them and beg them to let go of anything they think they know for sure, to welcome uncertainty, and to expect to be surprised. For everything that I thought I surely knew a year ago, perhaps only half of it still stands. My life is brighter and fuller, though, for letting the questions sweep me away.

Thank you for reading, and I hope you find your own questions to live.

All my love,

Julia

"Who is the happier man, he who has braved the storm of life and lived or he who has stayed securely on shore and merely existed?"

–HUNTER S. THOMPSON

Journal Entry,
August 11, 2009

Notes On Adulthood

1) It is expensive. Entirely liberating, though, to be fully in charge of your life and expenses.
2) What comes up must come down. One major score is often followed by a HUGE stumbling block. I think they call this character building.
3) You are ALWAYS forgetting something . . . some detail of importance in your life. I find that having a glass of wine makes you forget that you forgot something; thus, all better. This is not a problem, it is being a grown up . . . Sort of.
4) Your friends and family will become SO much more important to you than before. Suddenly people are the last thing in your life to be taken for granted . . . if you are smart.

I'm beginning to think that your twenties are for moving . . . always moving, both in your daily activities, and in the literal sense of moving between living situations. What better time, then, to learn to travel light? You don't need much . . . and you'll have great stories to tell your children one day.

I'm just barely into adulthood. In fact I don't even think of myself as an adult, but I'm expected to live as one so what are you going to do?

Maybe this is the key: to keep up with the expectations but always live a little bit as if you are a child in a grown-up world . . . the little girl playing dress up in her mother's heels. As long as you can make it across the room you are golden. And tripping here or there is just the beauty of the whole thing.

In short, my impression thus far of adulthood goes as such:

Learn to enjoy hard work. Live simply. Travel light. Relish people. Love deliberately and freely. Laugh whenever possible . . . and especially at yourself.

Lesson #1: Leap

I flew to New York on the day that Senator Ted Kennedy was laid to rest. I'll always have that locked in my mind. This sounds like it should contain within it some beautiful metaphor for life, for the journey at hand, yet no words can adequately express the raw sentiment of that moment. At twenty-two years old, I had decided to move to New York City on a hope and a prayer. I was naively optimistic and terrified at the same time. For months I'd been planning my escape. Young and single, I had nothing holding me back and was in the mood for a life-altering adventure. The time had come, today was the day; I was moving to NYC, and I was convinced I would never look back.

I had *some* money, money I'd spent four years saving, which sounds like it should be a lot, but it wasn't. A million dollars is a lot, and even that goes pretty fast in New York. I didn't have a million dollars. I didn't even have a fraction of a million dollars. I had *some* money . . . and that would have to do.

I had, in total, five large suitcases and a purse. That was my life, condensed into some 150 pounds. My life weighed more than I did, so that was nice; to know that your life weighs more than you. Again, it sounds like some nice metaphor, but I guess I'm no good with metaphors.

I remember my fellow passengers and I being pulled away from the airport televisions as the gate attendants tried to wrangle us to begin boarding. I remember feeling that this was such a monumental day in my life—and none of these other people knew it. These other people were just boarding another plane, but I was boarding The Plane. The Plane that was going to start this new adventure I had spent so long planning. The Plane that was going to deliver me to my new home. The Plane was ready to go and, strangely, I hesitated. For a second I wanted to run back through the gates, catch my parents before they drove off and tell them that it felt wrong, felt like a mistake. I didn't though, because that was fear talking. And I'd spent a fortune on all these preparations and, since I wasn't a millionaire, suddenly money became a very dictating force in my life. Plus I was excited . . . wasn't I?

I had made plans to crash for a night with a good friend who lived in the Village. I loved saying "the Village," like the locals said it. Like I knew what that meant or what area of town I was in or even what borough for that matter. I loved the feeling of zooming through the streets in the cab, directing him to go to such and such address, "It's in the Village."

"Yep, I'm staying in the Village for the night. Yeah, my friend lives in the Village. Sure! Let's go out tonight! I'm in the Village." I had arrived. Let the glamor begin.

This Village friend had warned me that she lived in a walk-up and I said, "Cool! Sounds great," which clearly shows I didn't know anything, especially what walk-up meant, because what it means is that when you arrive with your 150 pounds of luggage, you have to haul it up three flights of narrow stairs, and sometimes you drop it and it slides back down the stairs and then you are scrambling down after it and starting all over again, and clearly that isn't "cool" or "great." It is ridiculous. Like much of New York City is, as I would come to know.

It was good though. It was bone-rattling in its reality because here I was, having never spent any real time in this giant force of a city, yet I had showed up with my suitcases and my small bank account and said, "Here I am! I'm going to take this town by storm!" Which is, of course, the lie you tell yourself so that survival mode feels more like warrior mode; you chose this. *You* chose this earth-shaking reality for yourself so you might as well be optimistic about it and expect the very best. You pretend you are the bravest, most interesting and adventurous person that ever lived, rather than letting the truth sink in when you realize that this shit just got real, fast. I think it was in those first few hours in New York, after sweating like a pig hauling luggage up stairs and looking around and having no clue where I was or how I got there, that I realized that I had better get used to laughing at myself . . . often. I had better get used to having the best sense of humor in the world.

Lesson #2:
Cabbies Don't Know Brooklyn

I woke up the next day looking forward to schlepping my weighty life back down three flights of stairs and into a cab that was going to take me to my exciting new adult apartment in Brooklyn—because Brooklyn is where all the cool, artsy, and broke people live. I had tried to make myself look cute and trendy because, heaven forbid, anyone should look at me and know from my style that I'm actually from Ohio, and not a New Yorker in any way. Soon enough I'm carrying and dragging and pushing and dropping things down those stairs, and I'm sweating again, and I've been sweating ever since I got here anyway because these buildings are so old that none of them have central air. I look like a hot mess before I've even started my first full day. And in the end it doesn't matter anyway, because the first thing I see when I step out onto the street is some crazy bag lady wearing five fanny packs and one of those cartoonish umbrella hats. I suddenly realize this is a city where you get to let your freak card hang all out for everyone to see.

So I stand on the street and wave like an idiot while cabs fly by, and the bag lady thinks I'm waving at her, which is great, until finally my friend's mother, a true New Yorker, whips out one of those classic fingers-in-the-mouth whistles that stops traffic and, like magic, a cab pulls up. After plenty of hugs and "good lucks," I climb into the cab with all of my luggage and it's time to go to my new home. Another insane detail of this new adventure is that I had never actually seen the place that I had paid a small fortune in security deposit and first month's rent for. My roommate had found it and I was willing to accept anything, which is an unsettling truth to know about yourself—that you will just take anything in life.

In the back of the cab, fumbling with my new iPhone (also known as the magic phone) to find the address, I finally find it and tell the impatient driver that we are going to so-and-so street in Brooklyn.

Cabbie: Where is that?
Me: Ummm . . . it's at this-and-this on so-and-so street? . . .
Cabbie: I don't know where that is.
Me: Well me neither, you dumbass! I just moved here! I
   don't know what I'm doing with my life! I dropped half
   of my life savings on this mysterious address! I sold all of
   my clothes and favorite books so that what was left could
   fit in this little yellow car of yours, and I'm going to pay
   you the equivalent of two hour's wages for you to drive
   me there, and you are hardly speaking English to me, so
   would you just drive please? Just DO YOUR JOB?!?

That was actually just said in my head.

Me (in reality): Ok . . . umm . . . should you look it up?
Cabbie: You look it up. You have to direct me.

All of this is hardly comprehensible, by the way, because apparently now I'm in another country and English is not a viable language. Magic phone to the rescue! Activate map of the neighborhood that I apparently now reside in.

An awkwardly stressful thirty minutes later I pull up to my new building, settled on a charming, tree-lined street, and the excitement overrides the stress. I throw some dollar bills through the glass and haul ass out of the cab, sweating again as I clumsily unload the luggage from the trunk because Cabbie can't be bothered.

My faithful and true old friend from high school is there to help, but all she can think to do is try and take my picture because she says I'll want the memories. I just want to get inside. Just get me inside so that I know that it's a real place, a real apartment, and not a figment of my imagination.

And then it *was* real. I had keys that worked. I had a deadbolt to keep the creepers out. I had charming hardwood floors and high ceilings. It was HUGE! Look! I have a bedroom! Look! That little closet is the kitchen! How cute! Look how big the living room is! I could have dance parties in here!

> *Faithful Old Friend:* Well, the furniture will take up some room.
> *Me:* Damn. Forgot about furniture.

We got to work cleaning and unpacking and, of course, sweating. I blew up my name brand, double-sized air mattress and marveled at how, suddenly, the bedroom became a shoebox with the addition of a bed.

> *Faithful Old Friend:* You may want to have someone take a look at that.

Me: At what?

Faithful Old Friend: That water spot on the ceiling, the one right above your 'bed.'

Me: Oh, that's no big deal. I'll just drape scarves on the ceiling to cover it up or something.

Faithful Old Friend: Yeah . . . you may still want to have it looked at.

Cut to that evening: we're nestled cozily on pillows on the floor of the massive (but really not-so-massive) living room, huddled around my laptop to watch a movie with a cheap bottle of wine that I had purchased through bulletproof glass at the liquor store down the street, vowing never to walk that direction down the street again. Faithful Old Friend and I are giggling and feeling fun and young and adventurous when all of a sudden we see it, in unison, and simultaneously scream.

It was a tenant that had failed to vacate: a mouse. A sizeable mouse, darting through the kitchen, which was conveniently a mere twelve feet away from us.

We laughed. She reassured me that it was no big deal. I said it would be a good story to tell our future generations: "I had a mouse. I had a Brooklyn mouse." I thought, "Ok, I'm tough. No big deal, I'm not a wimp. Mouse in the kitchen—totally fine, I can catch one little mouse. I'm smarter than a mouse."

The mouse quickly became the least of my worries. Hours later, I was asleep on my bed of air, having a dream that I was swimming, or being splashed, or being swallowed by a hurricane. Halfway between sleep and consciousness, I thought perhaps the dream was just an incarnation of my fears and anxieties over the new chapter of my life. Then it got real, or I should say felt real: there was real water touching me. Real water dripping on my forehead, right between the eyes. I bolted upright in my bed, waiting for the wet sensation to end now that I was awake, but the drops slid down my forehead into my eyes. I looked upward to see water flowing through the crack in my ceiling. My bedroom ceiling was actually leaking, like a movie version of my own life. And of course, I had strategically placed my bed right below that leak, with my head catching each and every little droplet.

Seriously? SERIOUSLY?

I felt my blood pressure rising and my anxiety climbing to the point of a minor breakdown . . . and then I was just too tired to even get upset. So what did I do? I slid my air mattress to the other end of the shoebox-sized room and tried to go back to sleep. Day one in NYC and I'd already fulfilled two of the classic horror stories that people joke about when talking about New York City. So the journey began.

Journal Entry, September 2, 2009

Updates Concerning Mice and Leakage

To all those concerned:

- First, I know that "those concerned" is not many, because I know not many people read this. That is fine with me.
- Second, I am safely in New York. My use of "safely" is subjective.
- My bedroom ceiling leaks and there is a little friendly mouse that lives in my kitchen.
- I'm told all these things will be fixed. I'm skeptical, but content no less.
- There is a coffee shop down the street that is my new home away from home. If you know me, you know this is all I need to be happy in a place.
- I miss people, but am lucky to have people to miss.
- I live near (and I mean incredibly near) one of the most beautiful parks I have ever seen in my life. It is so big that I got lost walking through it today. If a park is so

large you can get lost in it, you know you are in a good place.

- The Mexican restaurant down the street has great sangria and killer black beans. Again . . . contentment.
- I have trees on my street. I am told this is rare here.
- I have no furniture. I sit on the floor. The apartment seems huge because of this. I still would rather have a place to put my fine ass. I need a futon ASAP.

All in all, things have gone smoothly. I know I'm in the right place. Transitions are tough, but I'll get there. Besides, these are the stories you tell your grandkids. No grandchild ever wanted to listen to their grandparents talk about that time when everything was wonderful and nothing went wrong.

Lesson #3:
Misery Loves Comedy

Yes, humor had certainly become the most important tool in my arsenal. Somehow, New York City lent to that. I wanted to claw my eyes out every time I heard that mouse scratching in the kitchen. One night though, I came home to find my roommate curled up on the couch in horror while she watched our superintendent try to catch the little bugger. Miguel was on his hands and knees, but when he stood up I almost choked on the laughter that tried to burst out of my mouth. This charming, older Dominican man was wearing Popeye pajama pants and fuzzy slippers.

"Eets jus a leetle mouse! Eet will no hurt ju!" he proclaimed.

My roommate and I thanked him for coming by so late, holding back laughter and avoiding each other's glances, knowing full well that we'd totally lose it if we looked each other in the eye. Miguel shook his head saying "Ju need anyting . . . ju know . . . ju call me. Anytime."

Oh we will Miguel, don't you worry, we sure will.

Without that mouse, we would never have seen Miguel's sweet-ass pajama pants, nor would we have had the laugh that followed his departure. Laughter trumps fear always.

My roommate and I laughed at the crazy characters we saw on the train. We laughed at how miserable we looked trying to lug groceries home on the train. We even laughed at my leaking ceiling and the scary bars that were on all our windows. In those first few days, when we were adjusting to everything, and frightened most of the time, laughter was our greatest and only defense, and I was lucky to have someone who found as much humor in the absurd as I did. So we laughed. When in doubt, just laugh it out.

Journal Entry,
September 7, 2009

I Have To Do It . . .

I've been putting off this entry for days now. I think maybe I just don't want to outwardly, publicly admit what I am about to admit. Pride may be to blame. Nonetheless, here it goes:

New York City is scary and overwhelming and I am homesick.

I said it. The truth is, when making a move like this, you prepare yourself for everything EXCEPT the emotional impact of such a change. Moving to NYC is like moving to another country in almost EVERY sense of the word. The pace of life is different. The timing is different (dinner at 9pm? what is that?). And don't even get me started on language barriers. I think English may actually be the outlier in this city. I run into a language/conversation barrier EVERYWHERE I go. Things like shopping take on a whole new meaning because you can't buy anything that you can't haul onto a train . . . or if you do you better factor in cab expenses.

On that note: cabs suck. Trains are much quicker and more

direct and cheaper. Cabs drive you in circles to run up the meter, and if you don't know NY backward and forward (who does?) then you would never know you are being taken advantage of.

Tonight, for example: I could have walked from where I was to the subway station in thirty seconds. I would have sat nicely and quietly for about twenty minutes on the train, and then five stops later I would have gotten off, walked approximately one minute, and been home. Instead, I had the brilliant idea to take a cab since it was late. The thing is, cabbies don't know Brooklyn. They DON'T. And I don't know Brooklyn beyond the block that I live on, and if I'm taking a cab, then I'm probably not a NY driver, so why are YOU asking ME for directions?

And then we hit the Caribbean Day Parade. Yep, I had totally forgotten that today (or the whole weekend) was National Caribbean Day. My neighborhood has a heavy Trinidadian influence. Basically, Carnivale was happening in my 'hood. I mean parade floats, costumes, the whole bit. Naturally, all the roads were shut down.

Our cab was stuck behind a giant sparkly peacock that was being rolled down the street by two guys on foot. My driver didn't know where to go or what to do, and he was shouting at two bikini-clad women to stop touching his car, so I had to get out and walk in an area that is much sketchier and much farther than the subway station would have been.

The thing is, you are in these situations (in the cab) and you are getting angry and frustrated . . . and then you realize that you are stuck behind a giant sparkly peacock. Only in New York.

So, after the cab ride from hell and the walk through Carnivale/Caribbean mayhem (where I was actually grabbed at by drunken men), it goes without saying that I was a little war-torn by the time I reached my building. I walked in my door and my lovely roommate had added little touches to our walls with personal messages. We had started a running tab of "What's Good?" What is good in the midst of all this mayhem? What in our life do we have to be thankful for? So she had started a list of "What's Good" on our wall.

A lot is good. That is what I need to remind myself of every day.

This city can get you down quickly, with little or no effort. Then you are reminded that you have friends and family that love you, and a passion in your life that drives you (that brought you to this crazy town in the first place). You see a man making a masterpiece out of sand, or a violinist on the subway platform just filling the void. A neighborhood of Caribbean immigrants who are spending the night remembering and celebrating the far-away home that they felt the need to leave. It's something special to say the least.

There is a lot of good; you just have to look for it.

Lesson #4: Not All Children Are Created Equal

In New York there are two types of actors: those who wait tables, and those who nanny. I guess some actors actually act and make money acting—but usually even that isn't true. If a twenty-something actor working in the theatre in New York tells you that they don't have another job, that their "full time job is just acting and auditioning!" it means they are trust-fund babies, or have a sugar daddy . . . or robbed a bank. Something along those lines. All of which is fine in my opinion, I just wasn't one of those lucky few.

I was the classic nanny actor. I had always worked childcare, I enjoyed childcare, and there is no money like the money you can make in childcare when you are a "starving artist" in NYC. I had found a family who had kindly put me on salary to work for them. Two kids, thirty hours a week; sounded like a piece of cake job to me.

On my first day of work I left with a black eye. You're right, I'm not telling the total truth. Though the two-and-a-half-year-old had, in fact, punched me in the face, it hadn't left me with a shiner. But the violent kicking to my legs definitely left bruises, and the fingernails slicing through my cheeks while he shrieked in my face had drawn blood—just a little though.

After just one day in this home with this family I felt . . . just . . . *wrong* about it all. When you get those gut-wrenching warning signals, you have to listen to them. I was having one of those and I didn't listen. That feeling was just a brief glimpse into what I would encounter over the coming year. A job that was intended to simply sustain me while I pursued my true calling would ultimately end up sucking me dry. All time, energy, and emotion drained. I know that now, but I didn't know that then. All I knew was that something was just not right. And that the toddler had a mean left hook.

A typical day would go something like this:

Riding the elevator up to the apartment, I would begin to talk to myself—"I am a talented and trained artist with a degree from the University of Michigan. What I do for money right now does NOT define me. I am a talented and trained theatre artist . . . "

Get to the door. Take deep breaths. "What, are you crying? *Stop* crying! Pull yourself together for goodness sake."

"Are you there, God? It's me, Julia. Could you please just fast-forward through this day?"

Me (finally entering the apartment after 20 minutes of pep talk):
GOOOOOD MORNING!

And thus it would begin:

Girl-child is lying on the floor, naked, rolling around and pounding her fists and screaming, "BUT I WANT IT" in the most ear piercingly loud manner. The kind that makes you want to rip your head off because that would probably feel better. Exactly the kind of noise I needed to hear at nine o'clock in the morning, after only sleeping six hours because I had worked until midnight the night before as well. Oh, and there's no coffee allowed because the parents *insist* it's bad for you and *insist* that I need to "get off of that stuff." Sure, great. Just perfect.

Meanwhile, boy-child would come flying by on his scooter, which he's not allowed to ride indoors (and he knows it). He also knows that he can ride around in front of me and provoke me, smiling a sneaky and manipulative smile that will make my spine shiver with fury. I'll try to discipline him, he'll start to scream, and then I will be the one left to look like an idiot and get scolded by Mom for not enforcing the rules. Part of me doesn't even want to catch him, because if I do, he will start the beatings and I just don't know how much more my body can take.

If I do catch the boy-child, he will go into his typical round of beatings (which will include punching, kicking, scratching and hair-pulling to name a few). Mom will then walk into the room and see all of this happening, only to deliver the most ineffective disciplinary tactic I've ever seen:

Mom: "Boy-child, hurting people hurts people . . . do we really want to do that?"

Wow. Thank you for that backup. I think he really took that to heart, considering he's now "playfully" choking me instead of scratching my eyes out.

Mom: "He's just having a hard time separating . . . you're just such a lover, aren't you boy-child! You just love your mommy!"

Boy-child, the "lover," is now biting my arms and calling me a "stupid idiot head."

Mom: "Remember, hurting people hurts people . . . "

Oh, thank you! That time it was more effective.

Mom: "Gotta run, I'm so late. HAVE FUN! Getting to play all day with sweet kids! What a fun job you have!"

No comment.

Journal Entry,
September 15, 2009

And If I Had A Shred Of Dignity Left . . .

My last shred of dignity flew off over the Hudson River as I pushed a red plastic tricycle down Fifth Avenue today. I have never felt so demoralized as I do on those days when the kids are a mess, and we are in public, and everyone is staring at the mess that we are, whilst I less than gracefully attempt to hurry us past the supermodels and beautiful people that are clearly living far more glamorous lives than me right now.

I listened to a brilliant speaker/pastor over the weekend who said something that really caught my attention. He said that we must stop looking AT where we are, and start looking FROM where we are. Now, we are always told and encouraged to live in the moment. This is true and good, I think, but also sometimes we get caught in the moment. It is so easy to stare at the ground around our current situation and forget to look up and out at the horizon. What does this moment have the potential for? We may not be exactly where we want to be in terms of career, relationships, financial assets, etc . . . but the moment we are in most certainly may be the launching point for something greater. I commute by train from Brooklyn into Manhattan every day, and I could stare at the ground or the wall . . . zone out and listen to my iPod and just get where I'm going and call that my morning commute. But when the train emerges from underground and comes across the bridge, if I pay attention, I get a spectacular view of the Manhattan skyline, the water, the Brooklyn Bridge, and (I learned today) the Statue of Liberty. EVERY DAY I get the chance to see this. What if I wasn't looking?

I am here. And from here, I can go forward, backward, or stay stuck. I'd like to think I'll go forward. This does not mean that who I am and what I am doing are invalid at this point. Rather, my current circumstance creates the platform for future success. I can complain about my job, but I have a job. And it got me to NY. What is there to complain about in that? The mere fact that it provides for me living here is opportunity enough.

I have my moments, daily, where I wonder what I have done with my life. And then I remember that I am young and free, that I have ambition and passion, and that I am living in an epicenter of the US. Amazing how I would still dare to be ungrateful under those terms.

I am Alice tumbling down the rabbit hole. Scary, crazy, but exciting nonetheless.

I have to say though, I look forward to the day when I don't have to walk past the Armani and Kate Spade stores, dressed in my $10 Forever 21 dress, pushing a tricycle while hollering for the two-year-old to "Steer! Steer!"

Lesson #5: Find The Music

In the midst of the culture shock of moving to this monster of a city, the thing I began to cherish was the surprises. I found that I was surprising myself daily with what I could do and what I was willing to try. I had somehow put on this coat of an adventurous spirit that I had never known I owned, and when I put on that coat in that city of twelve million people, I became this person that I had never met before. The City was seducing me and I was falling in love with the girl that I was there. My first major discovery was that I was a writer; this was something I had never considered myself before. My second discovery was that I would rather write than pursue anything theatre-related for a while, which was just fine because it wasn't like I'd just spent four years and $160,000 preparing for a career in theatre . . . oh wait.

Right as I'd moved to New York I had started a gig as a contributing writer for an online arts and entertainment magazine. Honestly, it was an easy way to get press access to shows and events that I would have never gotten into otherwise, and it was a good way to meet people. Yet, a whole new level of shamelessness appeared in my newfound bold spirit when I used the writing credentials for personal purposes: I used it to get to know a cute musician. It was the perfect pick-up line, perhaps the best pick-up line history has ever known:

"Hey . . . I'd love to write an article about you."

It happened so unintentionally, you have to believe me. I was going to meet Faithful Old Friend for a drink one of the first weeks I was in New York. Because it was one of my first weeks, I was still completely exhausted all the time. It took everything I had to pull myself off my air mattress that night and put on a half decent outfit to go meet her; it was truly the last thing I wanted to do. This is how life happens though: it's always in those moments of intense resistance that something pretty great usually shows up on the other side. The difference between something happening and something not happening is usually wrapped up in a split second decision, destiny being hinged on your choices. All of that to say, I hadn't wanted to go to the bar that night. However, when I walked in the door and saw The Musicians—I was *so* glad I'd gone.

The Musicians had a spark that I couldn't explain. There were just two of them, one on guitar and one on a ragamuffin drum concoction. They weren't performing a show for us, they weren't demanding attention or making an event of any kind; they were just playing. The strange thing was, as they continued to play in their casual, fun-loving way, people started paying attention. Before I knew it, the little Irish pub, that had been empty when I arrived, was full and vibrant. People were laughing and dancing and The Musicians were smiling and playing, taking just about any request we could throw at them. I had always been drawn to music; it was something that had always made me feel more comfortable wherever I was. That evening was the first time since moving that I had truly felt a sense of home.

When the evening came to an end my shoulders had lost that tense weight they'd been carrying. I smiled a tired smile as I dragged my heavy feet to the subway and back to the leaky ceiling and bed of air. In my hand I clutched a card with an email address and website for The Musicians . . . I knew what I had to do, shameful or not.

Journal Entry,
September 24, 2009

Life Is What Happens When . . .

Sometimes you end up somewhere you never expected, or even thought yourself capable of accessing. The surprising twists and turns are what make life what it is, though. I think we are better off when we stop trying to define and plan too ferociously and instead just follow our instincts toward our own happiness and capabilities. Perhaps good will come in ways you could never imagine for yourself.

Still though, you have to figure out a phrase to tell people when they ask, "What do you do?"

I think I'm going to start saying, "I am a storyteller." That is what it all is, isn't it? Every medium I work in is just telling stories. I don't have to settle or decide.

Lesson #6: You're Not Born Tough, Life Makes You Tough

A month or so in I was starting to hit a stride: I was riding high on the energy of the city, the movement of the tides of people. I would nanny by day and cover events by night. People I met in New York would refer to me as a writer, which was strangely satisfying as it was so far from what I'd ever imagined myself doing. There were these small, quiet moments that made me feel like I was in the midst of a great adventure, boldly walking through streets late at night just to see what I could see. I would ease my way into a small bar and sidle my way up onto the stools, order a glass of wine, and pull out a book or journal. I would smile a pleased little smile at the idea that I had become a person who could sit at a bar, alone, no fear. I always ended up meeting someone new and unique, engaging one another with interesting conversation before parting ways. These were people that I would most likely never see again, but it didn't matter because in those moments we shared this common thread of experience in having walked into a bar alone in NYC, and having decided to stay. And in having decided to stay, we met someone new and created an ounce of tiny little community which warmed us just enough to make it home.

I was amazed to find that the nights I went to bed most satisfied followed the days when I was closest to throwing in the towel. It was the greatest challenges that seemed to offer the greatest pay off. Plus, sometimes the absurdity of the challenges was just laughable. I remember one day when I pulled fourteen hours straight in nanny-land after working all day and night the previous day, grabbing a few quick hours of sleep in between before having to go back into the trenches for more. By the end of that second marathon day I was out of my mind, vowing to have my reproductive organs removed and swearing that I would quit nannying that very night, never to return. I had two different articles to write, I hadn't done anything creative in days, (which was a soul killer), and I had nothing but an air mattress to look forward to back in Brooklyn. This was not the life I had planned for myself. At midnight when I was finally relieved from my duties, having chickened out from quitting, I hauled my tired body onto the suffocating subway car and relaxed into the first empty seat I saw, happy that I could at least sit in peace for twenty minutes and listen to my music with no disturbance. But there was a disturbance. People were looking at me strangely . . . concernedly. I thought, "I know, I look tired. I am tired. This is New York, we are all tired." But the staring didn't stop and, in fact, I started to notice it was directed slightly to the left of me. I'd been blasting my music, not really paying attention to what was going on around me, but I could suddenly sense a faint disturbance in the force coming from the person whose elbows were rubbing mine, the person seated directly next to me. I dared to look . . .

And we had a puke girl.

It took everything I had in me not to laugh out loud. Not at her, of course. I felt terrible for her. She seemed like a sweet and unassuming, albeit terribly unlucky, young girl. She was periodically and systematically retching into a paper bag, enduring the glares and judging looks of our fellow passengers. Yes, I felt bad for her . . . but I wanted to laugh so badly. It had been the longest, most excruciatingly tiring and miserable couple of days that I had experienced in a very long time. I was looking at six hours of sleep at best before I had to go back into the misery of one more day. All I had wanted was to have my twenty minutes of peace on the train home— to listen to music and watch the Brooklyn Bridge pass by my window with the Manhattan skyline in the background. This was the moment I'd waited for, and of all the seats I could have chosen on that train car, I had picked the one next to puke girl. This is the kind of thing that I'm referring to when I say that I had to learn to laugh at everything. For me, that was my response to life throwing curveballs and roughing me up a little bit: I chose to laugh. It is undoubtedly gross to sit next to puke girl . . . but you have to laugh at that, even if it's just on the inside. Life will really get the better of you if you can't find these sour (no pun intended) opportunities to turn into comic gold.

Lesson # 7: Foreshadowing

Yet another thing was slowly developing in the midst of this new season of life: my friends and I had become Internet sensations. "Sensation" is a strange word to apply to oneself, but it was somewhat of a reality at the time. We had created a Harry Potter spoof musical and filmed it. They put it up on YouTube on a whim and it went viral. Suddenly people I'd never met wanted to be my friend on Facebook and girls everywhere were in love with my guy friends who I'd known forever. It was strange to say the least, yet exciting as well. I felt even stranger about it all because I was somewhat of a "spare" in the process: I had, in fact, not even been involved in the project initially.

It was the end of my senior year at Michigan and I had been directing my own show just a couple weeks prior to the impending Potter play. The two shows were rehearsing at the same time, and sharing many of the same actors, creating chaos, confusion, and stress in the way that only theatre people can. When my production came to an end, and *A Very Potter Musical* was just a few days away from opening, I came in one Sunday to help paint sets and was added to the cast at the last minute:

Director/Creator Friends: Umm . . . Julia? Do you want to
   be in the show?

Me: Ha ha, yeah that would be great guys. You're funny.

DCFs: No . . . we're serious.

Me: Wait . . . what?

DCFs: We never cast one of the parts. Do you want to do
   it?

Me: Wha . . . why? Why do you still have a part missing
   three days before the show?

DCFs: Ahhh . . . we screwed up. So you'll do it?

Me: Uh . . . can I really learn a three-hour musical in three
   days?

DCFs: (chuckling) Yeah . . . you're not that behind.

They were right. I wasn't that far behind, and those three
days were pure nonsense. But in the end we made something
pretty incredible, not even knowing then that it would turn
out to be something far beyond our imagination.

The strangest part of the sudden success of AVPM those
months later was being so far apart from one another as it
was happening. All of us spread across the country, pursuing
various endeavors, and ringing each other up to talk about
how crazy it all was. Out of necessity, the creative geniuses behind the project formed a company around AVPM, and thus
StarKid Productions was born. We'd always talked about
wanting to form our own company, to be able to create our
own work and do what we loved with the people we loved. It
had been a pipe dream, something fun to talk about, but
something we didn't really think could come to fruition. Perhaps we all had singular dreams and pursuits, but we always
ached a little to get back to one another. As the StarKid mania

was building (and would continue to build), there was no guess or expectation as to what could possibly develop out of this. At the back of my mind I secretly hoped it would change our lives. But until then, life had to go on as it was.

Journal Entry,
October 21, 2009

Is It Cold In Here?

I woke up this morning shivering under my thin, makeshift comforter. I did that awkward "I'm too cold to fall back to sleep, but also too lazy to get out of bed and put a sweatshirt on" dance, and then finally gave in and rolled over to close my window . . . tripping and tumbling over the bric-a-brac and stacks of books that constantly seem to surround my bed, no matter what city or state I'm living in.

I think it must be fall. I've been looking forward to my first fall in New York. I think it will be a good one. Fall always gives me a touch of the blues, but mellow blues . . . the kind you crave every now and again and just have to let yourself indulge in. I've got those certain songs I need to listen to, certain movies I have to watch. There are certain memories that I allow down off the shelf for a brief time, before stowing them safely back where they won't get in the way.

Autumn melancholy, though, is a tricky one; you don't love it, but you almost don't want to let it go either. This time of year for me is always full of wicked nostalgia: thoughts of all the wonderful people that have come and gone, or are coming and going in my life; too many people to keep up with, too many memories to miss. It's simply too much sometimes. It all unfolds as it will, but I think fall acts as a sort of memorial for me every year of all the things that I've loved, loved and lost, or just never had the courage to love at all.

Then again, when you take the time to remember them, the mistakes don't actually seem so rough anymore . . . and sometimes they even seem quite lovely from a distance. As for the people coming and going? Well . . . that's just life. I've found that when I let it roll through me it all goes much more smoothly, rather than clinging desperately to that which wants to move.

In other news, I laughed until I cried this morning, having a conversation with my roommate about lovers and loneliness and how to remedy that. The entire conversation was had through mouths full of granola and breakfast cereal, crumbs spewing from our mouths and greasy hair falling in our faces. Adorable. We may not be the cutest or best-dressed crayons in the box at times . . . but we know how to laugh. That is all I ask for in life.

Lesson #8: Duct Tape

By Halloween weekend I had been in New York for a very official sixty days. I had picked up a pattern of living that was similar to camping or backpacking. Despite paying a fortune in rent each month, I lived more like a squatter. I had never gotten around to getting a real bed; I was content enough with my big fancy air mattress. I didn't have a dresser or closet for my clothes (nor did I have room for one), so I pretty much lived out of a laundry basket on the floor. When I left my apartment each day, it felt like I was leaving on an epic journey. I would pack a bag full of food, water, a change of clothes, deodorant, toothbrush and toothpaste, makeup, and sometimes even a change of clothes. The magic phone became my map, personal assistant, and private guide all in one. Every day was like a trip into the jungle: I never knew what I'd encounter or where I'd end up so I'd better be prepared no matter what. It was exhilarating, but exhausting, and by the end of those long days the air mattress became the most important possession of my life—until one dreaded evening.

My bed, as I mentioned, pretty much took up my entire bedroom so I spent a lot of time literally in my bed. When I wanted to watch movies—I was in bed. Talk to people—in bed. Work on my writing—in bed. What happened that one dreaded night, though, still haunts me, and holds more embarrassment than I dare to share. All I'll say is: I was sitting in bed, and an accident happened. This accident included a stray spark that happened to land on the side of the mattress, burn through the sheet and then . . . Can you guess?

I watched it happen and then heard (and felt) it happen. Suddenly a loud gush of air started streaming out of the mattress. With that, the escaping air fed the spark that had burned through the mattress, causing the air to rush out and create more sparks. I, meanwhile, was swiftly sinking to the ground. I scrambled to protect my computer and books, wrapped and tangled in sheets and blankets and deflated mattress, watching fireworks shoot from the side of my now defunct bed. As quickly as it had started, it stopped. There I was, sitting in a pile of the remnants of my bed, embarrassed, exhausted, and not sure what to do next. It was around this time that I began the habit of talking out loud to myself, and to the God who I hoped was getting a bigger kick out of these moments than I was.

"Yep. Got it. No more candles by the side of the bed. But really? The bed?! The spark couldn't have just burned the rug? Seriously . . . the bed?!?"

And then I heard a voice clearer than any voice I'd ever heard. It was decisive; it was calming, it was clear. And that voice said two simple words:

DUCT. TAPE.

I leapt into action—a leap interrupted by the fact that I was netted awkwardly in the mess of fabric and plastic that a second ago had been my bed. So I guess you could say I tumbled into action. After a few minutes of unraveling, I was released from my web of shame and ready to put that magic repair system to the ultimate test: I was going to fix my bed with duct tape. I was going to have victory over this karmic event and I would then sleep peacefully knowing that I was the MacGyver of my own life.

In the end, duct tape wasn't enough. But when I super glued the duct tape over the hole, victory was mine. Take that you limp air mattress! I win! Now you have to hold air for me and let me sleep on you every night! Bet you thought I'd throw you out and get a real mattress, huh? No such luck! I'm keeping you! I win! You lose!

Until I realized that I was talking out loud to my haphazardly repaired air mattress. Then I started to wonder if I was the one losing . . . losing my mind.

Journal Entry,
October 31, 2009

Sixty Days

That is the number. Two Months. For sixty days I have lived in NYC. I am seduced, to be sure. I am mesmerized. I am bewitched. Yet, sixty days is a vacation. I feel more like I've been camping here for a bit. Perhaps I will put down real roots . . . but perhaps not. I don't know. But here is my sixty days update:

- My bedroom ceiling began to leak AGAIN. This time, it was like Lake Placid. The floor and towel were soaking wet and bowls were filled. My daily routine now incorporates the calling of the Super to see when things will be fixed. You slide your bed over and deal, I guess. This is camping. These are the stories of your life.
- Tonight my air mattress sprung a leak. It was completely my fault, I won't go into detail, but my bed deflated within a matter of minutes. I suffocated it with packing tape to the extreme and attempted a re-inflation. I can still hear a faint whistle of air escaping, and I expect that

I will wake up on the ground, mattress fully deflated. I'll deal. New York makes you strong in ways you wouldn't expect.

- I am inspired everywhere, yet missing the resources that came with my artistic family and home in Michigan. Here, I am ready to create things every moment of the day, yet the process is complicated and unknown. In Michigan, daily life was blasé, but the access to people and opportunity was unlimited. Such a catch-22.

Things I miss about the Midwest:

- Driving. I used to drive for hours through back roads simply for enjoyment's sake. Now the idea of a car is so foreign to me that I would almost be afraid to get behind the wheel again. I miss late night car rides with good friends; getting picked up on a first date; the freedom that came with knowing you had keys and a vehicle waiting to take you anywhere you chose. Yet I never went far . . . tricky.
- Neighborhoods. By this I mean traditional, Midwest neighborhoods. There is something about driving down a charming street that you have known for years, with neighbors waving, that just makes you feel like you belong to something. Kids jumping in leaf piles and selling lemonade, neighbors shaking their heads as my car enters its sanctuary with music blasting and windows down, and block parties and cookouts. It all just gives you that old fashion feel of down-home living. I miss that.
- Cheap drinks.
- Home gatherings. People don't really hang out in each other's "homes" in NY. But I miss hosting dinner parties,

and attending dinner parties, and just spending time with people in relaxed settings. Bars are fun, but sometimes you just need a low-key night with good people in a relaxed environment. This, to me, is Midwest entertaining at its best.

- Stars. I don't want to talk about it. You can't see a single star in this city. Cincinnati definitely had light pollution, but at least I got SOMETHING. And if I REALLY wanted to see some good stuff, it was a quick drive and I knew where to go. How do New Yorkers live without seeing the stars?

I owe it to New York to say that I am most assuredly enamored. The access to such great things and the constant energy is exhilarating. But I am an American girl, tried and true. I miss my football games and my neighborhood cookouts. I miss the simplicity of days and long, late night drives through foliage and winding roads. I miss lakeside vacations and camping. I miss that touch of country that manifests itself in everything.

But I am here. And I am happy I am here. I am a Midwestern girl who picked up and moved to NYC, because she believed there was just a little more life to be lived. I wouldn't trade anything for the experiences I am having now, but I also wouldn't change my upbringing in the slightest way. We are who we are, and we are shaped by what we are shaped by. I am an American, Midwestern girl through and through.

Lesson #9:
Quarter Life Crisis

For the first two months of my great new adventure, I pride-fully hid under the excuse that I was still exploring and set-tling in. I didn't have a plan, but I didn't need one; I was just settling in. I was learning how to navigate. I was getting com-fortable with the kids I took care of. I was exploring how to be a writer. I was meeting new people. I was settling. After Halloween, though, it didn't seem fair to use that excuse any-more. The logistics of life were figured out: I was paying my bills, I had a "bed" to sleep on, I had a daily routine of sorts, and I had friends. I had spent months and months panicking about how those ducks were going to line up. I tossed and turned for months before the big move in sheer terror as to how I was going to make money, pay bills, and generally just provide for myself. What no one tells you, though, is that those are usually the easier parts of the equation. Those are the basic necessities. If you are a smart, competent, decently hard-working person you will find a job, you will meet your simple needs. Once those are met you have no excuses any-more . . . you have to face the big scary question:

What do I want to do with my life?

I think it is easy in this country to fast-track people toward an answer to that question without really looking at all of the details involved. When we are merely fifteen, we have to start looking at colleges, and in looking at colleges we need to know what kind of program we want to go into and thus what we want to "be when we grow up." We graduate high school, go to college, and for four years put blinders on and intensely study some skill or trade that we plan to make a life out of. But twenty-three-year-old me is so different and more informed than fifteen-year-old me. Do I want to be an actor? Yes . . . until I take a look at the lifestyle of an NYC actress and then it just doesn't seem as tempting. Do I want to be a director? Yes. Yet, I don't know that I can wait twenty years to actually do what I want to do. I certainly know that I will die if I have to nanny for twenty years. Do I want to be a writer? Yes. Especially right now, yes. I know, though, that writing will never fulfill me in a lifelong sense. So what the hell do I want? What do I want to do? What drives me, inspires me? What legacy do I want to leave? And most importantly, what do I want my life to look like? What quality of life, what quantity of life, and who do I want to share it with? What do I want this life to be?

Yes. Those are the tough parts. Waking each day faced with those looming question marks buzzing around your head like gnats in the hot summer. I had been having a decent enough time in New York up until that point but I wasn't contributing a single thing. I wasn't using the parts of me that I wanted to. I didn't feel that buzz, that drive that I'd come to know and love so well. I ached for the times when my projects had been so all encompassing and inspiring that food and sleep became uninteresting and unnecessary. I ached for some purpose, something driving me to get up every day. I craved something that was bigger than me. The honeymoon was over. It was time to get focused and get a vision for what I wanted to do next.

It was around this time that I began to truly go crazy. I would have arguments with myself in my bed at night. I would mumble under my breath while I was making lunch for the kids. I was mulling it over, chewing on the desires of my own soul. I'd make excited phone calls home to very confused and worried parents:

> *Me:* I love writing! I really enjoy it, and I'm good at it! I want to do this; I bet I could have a career in this!
> *Parents:* Great! Then go do it.

(A week later)

> *Me:* I had this incredible realization last night! I love acting! I still want to be an actor! I miss it so much and I'm talented! And trained! Why shouldn't I act?
> *Parents:* Absolutely. That is what we paid all that tuition for after all! Go do it.

(An hour later)

> *Me:* I've decided. I definitely want to be a director. Directing is like jumping out of an airplane, it's so thrilling! I can't give that up.
> *Parents:* For God's sake then GO DO IT! Julia, you just have to do *something*.
> *Me:* But sometimes I think I want to just travel and explore for a while, maybe I just need to take time and relax, enjoy New York. I mean I've really gotten into this music scene and . . .

Parents: We're hanging up now. We support whatever you want to do as long as you're happy. But for goodness sake just choose something and go for it.

Me: WAIT, WHAT ARE YOUR THOUGHTS ON MAR-RIAGE AND CHILDREN?!?!

CLICK.

Even my parents couldn't handle the crazy. The next evening I was walking down Fourteenth Street after a long day of uninspiring, mind-numbing childcare. I walked, talking to myself, protected from shame under a cover of darkness and other crazy mumblers. My fists were shoved deep into my pockets, my fingernails digging into my palms as I quietly but intensely debated my life options with myself and the pavement below me. Out of the corner of my eye I caught a glimpse of jerky movement. Looking up I saw a man jumping back and forth in front me as he headed my direction, waving, trying to block my path or get my attention. Far enough away that I couldn't make out a face yet, I stiffened in anticipation of a very typically awkward encounter with a very common crazy bum. I started to nod my head as if to say "not today guy, please, just not today," yet as I took two steps closer the unidentified face went from unsettling to heart-thumping in a beat: it was one of The Musicians. The Cute Drummer. The one I had been pretending not to have a schoolgirl crush on for the past two months.

Journal Entry,
November 12, 2009

Conversations With Myself

I've had a gaggle of conversations with myself lately. A whole boatload. A sinking Titanic ship full of screaming, drowning conversations . . . With. My. Self. Fantastic.

So I'd like to re-create one of these said conversations here, with the aid of my two wonderful acting pals, Logical Julia and Crazy Julia. No judgment should be placed on these dear friends due to their names . . . they each hold equal, if not EX-TREMELY different, merits and values to me. Anyway, we commence:

Logical Julia: So I am settled now. I need to start being more productive, what are we going to do next?

Crazy: Ooh Ooh! We should travel! Let's travel!

LJ: We just moved here . . . we're not moving again.

C: That is a dumb reason! We are young! We are supposed to be moving all the time and exploring!

LJ: We can explore NYC. We might as well be in another country. Besides, we have things to get done here.

C: Oh yeah! Ok, so I dig the writing thing but I think that we need to get up and perform again. Ooh! And also direct! I want to direct again! And remember that dream we always had about . . .

LJ: Whoa, I can't even hear your inane ramblings you are talking so fast and excitedly.

C: Don't be mean to me just because I'm the creative genius in this pairing and you are boring.

LJ: IT'S NOT BORING . . . IT'S LOGIC. It will get you through life.

C: WRONG! And boring.

LJ: Ok, then you tell me what our next step is here, eh?

C: Ooh! Ooh! Well we need to act again, that's a must. I miss theatre. OOH! And maybe we could take a road trip! Maybe we could film a documentary road trip! Like *This American Life*! On Film! Ryan Gosling should be our travel buddy. So sexy. I also want to do *Summertime* again, do you want to direct that show again? I loved that show and also . . .

LJ: You are hurting my brain.

C: What are you thinking about marriage, by the way? See, I'm thinking we should meet someone right away and then have this awesome partner in crime while we do all of our awesome things. Like, we should get married NOW! How cool is that?

LJ: Umm . . . less cool, more awkward and terrifying. Why would you want to get married?! You can't even commit to a sandwich choice . . . or a career path.

C: I have a career path! I am an artist!

LJ: Awesome. That is completely specific and helpful.

C: Hey we should have a TON of kids too. I love kids.

How cool is it going to be to have kids one day? We should just create this huge, cool, artsy family!

LJ: Yeah . . . we're not having kids any time soon. You have enough trouble remembering to feed yourself. We don't even have a fish.

C: Let's get a fish. NO! OOH OOH! LETS GET A TURTLE!! I WANT A TURTLE.

LJ: Oh, it's like bugs in my ears, the words that come out of your mouth sometimes.

C: Ok, but back to the serious conversation we were having . . .

LJ: Some part of this conversation was serious?

C: So I think this is what life should look like for us. We'll open up that cafe/bar we always wanted to. By day we will write whatever we are writing, or rehearse whatever we are rehearsing. By night we will perform, or invite friends to perform at the bar. We will pick a month each year that is devoted to travel. And we'll set up a playpen in the corner of the bar where the kids can hang . . . throw 'em a biscuit every once in a while.

LJ: That is completely . . . wait. That's actually not so bad. Don't know how we will get there . . . but that actually sounds quite nice.

C: And we can hang all of our artwork on the walls so it finally gets seen!

LJ: No. Those aren't for show. They are for fun. They are no good.

C: IT'S OUR BAR!

LJ: Up for discussion later. One more thing . . . final consensus on the marriage/kids thing?

C: It happens when it happens . . .

And that one took place in the privacy of my own bed-room. The real danger comes when they start up while I'm on the train or in the streets. Luckily, in NY, even the crazies like me don't look all that crazy in comparison.

Lesson #10: Chin Up,
Or You'll Miss The Surprises

As I mentioned, I'd seen the infamous Musicians during my first week in the City. They had filled my tired, empty heart and put a smile in my stomach. Wanting so badly to simply connect with people, and to connect with people that had that spark, I had pulled out a new weapon and contacted them after that night to set up an "interview." Thus, we met, and I wrote about them, but more importantly I became a regular. They were kind to me. I went to listen to them almost weekly with friends and they knew my name, came to know my friends, chatted, smiled, played our requests, made us laugh and made me feel like "living the dream" wasn't such a ridiculous request. Mr. Guitar was older, proudly married, and so young at heart. He was thankful and complimentary of any coverage I could give to them. He was so excited and proud of his life and his work. He was happy. Drummer Boy was the smiliest man I'd ever seen. When he played, I swear fireworks shot from his drum kit; he couldn't have been more full of joy. He was pretty damn attractive and charming too, I might add.

At times I felt like a groupie of sorts, something that I

hated the idea of for all its foul-tasting connotations. I couldn't stay away though. I couldn't put my finger on it, but when I sat in on their sets—surrounded by their other musician friends, watching them jump in and out, rotating like a tribe with an other worldly connection—when I was in the presence of that I thought, "Yes! This is what I want! This is what I crave . . . an artistic family. An artistic home."

So when Drummer Boy leapt into my path that evening on Fourteenth Street—laughing at the intensity with which I'd been walking down the street and then chatting easily about my life, his life, what was happening around that night and would I come to their gig down on Bleecker—in that moment of such familiarity on a chilly and lonely evening I relaxed a little. I allowed a smile. I said of course I'd go watch them play. I let go of any anxiety over how cute or not cute I looked to the Drummer (who I didn't have a crush on, of course) and I let go of any worry over being seen as a groupie. I had been caught by a pleasant surprise in a solitary state after a soul-sucking day, and if I wasn't careful, I was going to miss more wonderful surprises just like that one. Face to the pavement in conversation with only my own mind is no way to live at all. I wasn't going to have all the answers that night or the night after for that matter. So I might as well enjoy myself for an evening and take a break from the confusion. Like a moth to the flame, then, I went.

It was crowded but I wiggled my way through the people to find my place. I gleaned a quick moment of pride at the discovery that I wasn't afraid to walk into a crowded room where I didn't know anyone. For a person that has always been blessed with many friends and an adventurous outgoing spirit, I had also always been a person who was afraid to go it alone. I didn't like showing up places alone, I didn't like standing in crowds alone. Yet, I stood there alone and felt confident and proud of myself. Small victories.

When a table opened up I swept over and set up camp, tucked in where I could watch and enjoy The Musicians inconspicuously. Out of the corner of my eye I spied two tall men searching for a place to squeeze their large frames. Before I even realized what I was doing, I told them they could share the table with me, that I was there alone and didn't need all four seats after all. They happily sat and offered me a drink in return for my generosity. It wasn't creepy, like all the stories you are warned of when moving to a big city, it was just common courtesy between strangers. Again, I was surprised at my own confidence and bravery. Yes, it seems so small but for me it felt so huge: to have gone to a place where I knew no one, to sit at a table alone, to offer my empty seats up to a couple of strangers. It was not the Julia I had known. "This must be me growing," I thought to myself. The tourists (from South Africa, I would come to find out) asked me did I live here, and when I said yes they gawked in awe and admiration. How lucky I was, they said. They asked what I did and did I know the musicians and I said yes, I wrote for them and had become friendly with them. So I was a music journalist, they declared. How fascinating! Suddenly, sharing what I thought to be the most mundane details of a life I was currently dissatisfied with became exhilarating and cool in the eyes of these tourists. In their minds, my life was hip and glamorous. We enjoyed an evening of music and I felt their eyes on me in wonder as I went up to the guys after the set and said hello. As we chatted, I was introduced to other musician friends of theirs and made plans to meet and interview more people.

I walked out that night into the chilly yet bustling Village, bowing my head not in frustration, but in gratitude to a God who I felt was reminding me to put things in perspective. Life was not all bad. In fact it was quite good in moments like that. If you spend all of your time focusing on what isn't working in your life, you lose a lifetime of moments that *are* working, that are wonderful and singular which you can never get back if you miss them.

I rode the train back to my little Brooklyn campsite and made sure to catch the magnificent view of the skyline as we went above ground and across the bridge. As I walked down my tree-lined street I felt the urge to look up. There were stars in the sky in Brooklyn that night, and a perfect crescent moon. It wasn't whole, but it was bright. The stars were few, but those few were fighting their way through the light pollution to be seen. I felt a glimpse of promise return.

Journal Entry,
November 19, 2009

Namaste

I can tell you one thing for sure . . . New York will whip the hippie right out of you. Mine is too deeply rooted, though. She isn't going anywhere anytime soon.

My last seventy-two hours have gone a little something like this: overwhelming fear; incredible homesickness; loneliness beyond redemption; confusion; denial; depression; anxiety; nostalgia; regret. And the Ugly Cry. Oh hell yes, the Ugly Cry.

What was that all about? I consider myself to be a more than generally optimistic person. But I went to the dark place this week. One can never quite be sure what it is that triggers such surges of despair . . . they usually (at least for me) seem to come seemingly by surprise. In my journey of spirituality and faith, I have come to believe that the darker forces in the universe will gravitate toward the light. Or maybe it is that when we are on the brink of our own greatest discoveries and lightness, we put the brakes on and get in our own way out of fear, drawing our own worst nightmares into our proximate consciousness. Bottom line . . . I think that bad stuff comes to the surface right when we are about to break free from it for good.

The point of entry for it all in me seems to be this one, all-encompassing fear: for the first time in my life, I'm not exactly sure where my life is headed. In this, I mean that suddenly my one lifeline and passion has multiplied into three, so I am left with confusion. I am away from everything and everyone that shaped me. I feel homesick in a way I have NEVER felt homesick before. I have felt loneliness in a way that is mind numbingly painful. And I guess I hit a point where I saw my life playing out as a series of days full of these terrible feelings, with nowhere to go, and no one nearby to love or be loved by.

The REAL truth, though? The universal truth that I have experienced in my life year after year? I am being taken care of. I have always drawn the most amazing, fascinating, talented, and loving people around me . . . no matter what city I am living in. That HAS always been true, thus it will always be true. Namaste. I respect and trust that knowledge . . . I have faith in that knowledge.

I have ALWAYS found myself in exactly the location I was meant to be in at exactly the right time. Even my failures created my greatest, most abounding successes. That has always been, thus it will always be. I am exactly where I was intended to be, and this moment plays an important role in the story I am telling. I AM BEING TAKEN CARE OF. Thus, I don't have to understand the purpose or reason for this frustration or confusion . . . all I have to do is learn how to harness its power. I can choose fear or love. And hippie that I am, I will always choose love. Namaste. I respect and trust this awareness and knowledge. I have faith in the awareness.

Loneliness is a state of mind. If I believe (and I do) that we are all connected, then I am no lonelier than the stars are in a blanket of sky. Beyond that, I am genuinely blessed with friends in dozens of cities all across this country and world, a family that offers unwavering support, and a system of people who never cease to surprise and amaze me with their love and devotion toward my happiness.

Who the hell am I to be depressed? I have been BEYOND blessed my entire life. So in this moment I could either choose to believe that my luck has run out—and that would be my choice—thus, I would reap those consequences. Or, I can choose to have faith in the understanding that nothing is just luck or coincidence, that my life has not been a string of beautiful moments for nothing. My journey has not been futile. My purpose has yet to be fully realized, therefore . . .

The best is yet to come.

I think at the root of it all is the decision that happiness is worth being the one single pursuit in your life. Everything else is just means to an end. My intent from here on out is the constant and vigilant pursuit of joy and happiness. Everything else falls in line from there. I could give you a million things that I want to see happen in my life, that I want to accomplish, that I want to pursue. I don't know what is next, though, and I have to allow myself the freedom of not knowing. I am being taken care of. My commitment need only be to listen, to remain open, and to work my ass off when the opportunities present themselves, AND NOT A MOMENT BEFORE. After all, working fruitlessly and blindly just for work's sake does no one any good. I have fallen victim to this too many times in my life, and all it does is leave me too exhausted to work hard at, and for, the good stuff.

The end of this story (or is it the beginning?) is that I am on the journey of life, and I am on it now. I am committed to finding joy in the immediate, and I refuse to live in constant preparation for whatever will be the next great phase. It's over when it's over, kids. But it ain't over UNTIL it's over.

I'm really into humbling myself to ask for help lately . . . I think it is a powerful act. I humble myself by writing this, by admitting that I don't have it all together, I am not sure and confident in every step of the way, and I need people more than the desert needs the rain. But I do know that even when I am not happy, I remain fully committed to my faith in and pursuit of joy and purpose . . . so I will never truly be lost.

Lesson #11:
Oh Yeah . . . Kids

So I was having all these beautiful discoveries about my soul and myself. I felt adventurous and sassy. I chatted with strangers and flirted with music and reminded myself to be thankful for the stars and the moon and the bright city lights. Let us be quite clear though . . . I was still a nanny. Just a nanny. My money came from potty training and picking up toys. I woke up each morning in a dreary apartment that I somewhat despised and put on clothes that I felt could withstand the blows and pulls of angsty children . . . while attempting to look somewhat presentable in a city obsessed with appearance.

As we entered into the season leading up to Thanksgiving, I had gotten to what felt like a decent place with the family and the kids. The mother seemed to trust me, and suddenly she would shower me with little presents and bonuses. In theory, that was great. In actuality, it was unsettling. I never knew what mood to expect when I walked through the door each day. Was she going to worship at my feet of nanny greatness? Or would she berate and scold me, passive aggressively convincing me that I was the worst caretaker to ever step foot in the land of NYC Nanny-dom? She was inconsistent, had been from the beginning. I hated blaming her, because I saw so much stress and anxiety in the family that was beyond her control, yet I caught myself taking on the troubles of the brood and letting it affect me in my off-hours . . . and I knew that was a bad path to go down. There were days when I put every ounce of energy I had into creating wonderful worlds of creativity and imagination for the children to play in. We painted pictures of imaginary worlds, made blanket forts and incredible paper airplanes . . . only to have them stomped on later when one of the parents came home and was unhappy with the way I had aligned the shoes by the entryway. The days when I walked away feeling bad at my "job" were the worst because I knew I could do this . . . I could take care of kids. You can judge my acting, you can correct my directorial skills and you can edit my writing, but to tell me that I am bad at childcare? At the job that is meant to just sustain me rather than swallow me? That is just unacceptable. To walk away from a day's work that was already unfulfilling, and then feel like I was even bad at *that* was the worst feeling I'd ever encountered.

I saw the pattern of caretakers being caught in impossible circumstances. These were difficult children; stubborn, spoiled children acting out in unimaginable ways whilst the nannies attempted to discipline and still preserve their jobs. We would share knowing glances during playdates. We would hesitantly express certain frustrations, never knowing how much we could trust one another not to gossip to our bosses, yet knowing that we were all struggling with the same things. Being a nanny was a major element of my life at that time. It was an all-encompassing element. Being a nanny in New York City was a game I hadn't trained for. The society I was running in was a realm I hadn't prepared for.

First, let's explain playdates: they are the equivalent of "drinks with friends" for four-year-olds. Playdates are also the social negotiations of parents who want to climb the ladder of the community. If the kids are friends then the parents *have* to be friends, so playdates became a primary way for parents to get ahead socially. One day I was instructed to take the kids to a playdate, only to show up and find myself in Annie Leibovitz's house. "What? What the hell!?" I'm trying to monitor the kids, but dear God, there is a picture of John Lennon on the wall! No one thought to warn me that this was where I would be spending my day? In the beautiful four-story West Village brownstone of one of the most admired and celebrated photographers in celeb-dom? No wonder the parents were stressed; they were keeping up with the Leibovitz's. They were a beautiful, ordinary family trying to be extraordinary in a circle of people who represented NYC's elite. They were fighting for their five-year-old to get into the most prestigious (and might I add, expensive) schools in the city . . . for kindergarten. They were going to pay more for her years in primary school than my parents had spent for my entire education, kindergarten through college.

Girl-child, age five, was a special, beautiful child. She was one of the magic ones. She could create whole worlds full of characters and creations that she would enact and perform for an audience of one: herself. Adults would get frustrated with her for not listening, not paying attention, not focusing. I was one of the guilty parties, so caught up in the task of wrangling these kids that I would miss the magic—until I saw and recognized that glazed look in her eyes that stopped me in my tracks. I knew that look . . . she was in her own world of her creation and couldn't be bothered with our petty talk. I too had done that as a child and throughout my growing years, and I still do it now. It is the best feeling in the world—to be able to create such wonderful imaginings that the reality before you becomes an unimportant bother. Girl-child was being smothered by tutors, piano teachers, and voice lessons, all attempting to "foster her abilities," but what she wanted, what she needed, was to be left to her own wonderful devices. She was drowning in kindergarten entry tests and interviews. Her soul was being beaten down . . . and I saw myself in her. I was the most unfair to her on the days that I felt most stricken down. She wanted to imagine and dream and play and create . . . and I, too, wanted that. I wanted nothing of this new adult incarnation of myself. Paying my bills, cleaning, working meaningless hours to fill my bank account. I saw the reality of a dead-end job; working for something that would lead me nowhere, for something that would leave nothing for me. No legacy to speak of. I wanted to play again. I craved the magic.

Girl-child didn't want to be known for having gotten into the best kindergarten, or having been the smartest child to take the entry exam. She wanted to be known for the beautiful characters that she fancifully created and tried to bring to life in her bedroom. One day I was reading Dr. Seuss to her, curled up next to her in her bed, and I found myself weeping pathetically because I saw myself in that five-year-old. Though she had little control of her circumstances, I theoretically had all the control, yet I was doing nothing about it. I chose to sell myself to a slavery of sorts day after day, and I chose to have a bad attitude about my life and my possibilities. This little girl made my gut wrench with realization that this was my life now, and I was the only one that could make things happen for myself. Her parents and teachers, and even I, dictated girl-child, but whom was I dictated by? Truly?

I was dictated by me. I was dictated by me, myself, and my actions. So, if I was unhappy, what was I doing to change it? Nothing. I was waking each day expecting a miracle, yet doing nothing different from what I'd always done. I was avoiding the room that facilitated my dreams and ambitions. I was doing the same thing day after day and expecting different results—the definition of insanity.

Journal Entry, November 21, 2009

A Quote From Vincent Van Gogh

"To be good—many people think that they'll achieve it by doing no harm—and that's a lie, and you said yourself in the past that it was a lie. That leads to stagnation, to mediocrity. Just slap something on it when you see a blank canvas staring at you with a sort of imbecility.

You don't know how paralyzing it is, that stare from a blank canvas that says to the painter you can't do anything. The canvas has an idiotic stare, and mesmerizes some painters so that they turn into idiots themselves.

Many painters are afraid of the blank canvas, but the blank canvas is afraid of the truly passionate painter who dares—and who has once broken the spell of 'you can't.'

Life itself likewise always turns towards one an infinitely meaningless, discouraging, dispiriting blank side on which there is nothing, any more than on a blank canvas.

But however meaningless and vain, however dead life appears, the man of faith, of energy, of warmth, and who knows something, doesn't let himself be fobbed off like that. He steps in and does something, and hangs onto that, in short, breaks, 'violates'—they say.

Let them talk, those cold theologians."

Lesson #12:
You May Travel Far, But Always Find Your Way Home

Thanksgiving came, and not soon enough. Miss Independent was homesick. Terribly homesick. I missed simple comforts like a real bed, heat that worked, fresh food, and an abundance of space. I also missed the more complex indulgences that I'd once taken for granted: people who knew me and had known me forever; hugs from the people who loved me; and passing words of support and encouragement from these people.

I cried for three days straight leading up to that trip home. In true New York fashion, though, I was blindsided in the midst of my misery by a beautiful, classic night out. My two best friends, who had become my partners in crime in this crazy town, were always up for a little celebration, if only to distract us from the scarier things we faced. The night before my trip back for Thanksgiving, the three of us pulled an all-nighter. We laughed and danced with our musicians in a tiny pub on Mac-Dougal Street. We bounced down to the Lower East Side to stop in on a new musician and let her huge voice blow us away. We walked through the crisp night, stopping in our favorite all-night café for two o'clock breakfast and goofiness. Before we knew it, it was four o'clock in the morning and time for me to get in a cab and head to the airport for that flight I'd been so looking forward to. I suddenly forgot why I'd been so unhappy, and why I'd been so desperate to get back home.

As we began our descent into Cincinnati, though, I could feel the tears prickling behind my eyes with the anticipation of seeing my family at last. Despite their best efforts to hide it, I knew that my parents spent many waking hours thinking in sheer terror of where I was living and what I was attempting to do. Mostly, they could read through my brave voice on the phone and they knew that I was struggling . . . my parents knew that I simply wasn't really happy and that was hard on them. If I had walked out of security and collapsed into an emotional pile of tears, begging them not to make me go back (which is what I wanted to do), I'm pretty sure it would have sent my mother into a total nervous breakdown. Yep, no one needed that. Big girls don't cry, or so they say. So I put on my armor of strength, the one that I dutifully put on just about every day, and I walked out smiling. I knew that even three days of sheer bliss with my family was a blessing that I should enjoy fully and be thankful for, because it could be worse. If I had not had a family or home to return to, I don't know what I would have done. As I mentioned before, the people in your life suddenly become monumentally more important than ever before. I have never been more thankful for the home that I had to return to than I was that Thanksgiving.

All too quickly I found myself back at the airport for my return flight to New York. It was nothing like that first flight I had taken almost three months ago, the one that began the journey. It was the same airport, the same gate even, but a completely different energy. The minute I was out of my parent's sight the tears began. I didn't even have the energy to be embarrassed at being so publicly emotional so I simply let myself cry. For the first time, though, I really pondered the worth of all that I was doing, if the idea of returning to NYC filled me with such dread. I always told myself that these feelings would pass, that a little homesickness was normal. How much do you put up with though, before you make the decision that something has to change?

Journal Entry,
November 25, 2009

The Dreaded Feast

It is four thirty in the morning on the Wednesday before Thanksgiving, and I am huddled over my laptop at LaGuardia Airport. I have now been awake for approximately twenty hours, and have hours, and many miles, to go before I sleep. I am homeward bound for the holidays, and to keep me company I have some well-known writers and their tales of holiday gloom and woe: *The Dreaded Feast: Writers on Enduring the Holidays*. The combination of the flickering florescent lights, the lack of sleep, a jittery caffeine-induced buzz, and the words on these pages is creating a false sense of terror and dismay for me in this eerily quiet airport.

As I finish up a story written by Chris Radant about her torturous journeys home for the holidays each year, I am disrupted by the angry shouting of this morning's token crankster; apparently she is none too happy that our flight has not begun boarding yet. It is clear though, that nothing would make this woman happy. They could announce that to apologize for the delay, this morning's flight will come with a gourmet breakfast cooked on the plane while we are serenaded by Josh Groban singing Christmas carols from the tenth row, and she would STILL throw a fit that we aren't boarding yet. I wonder if perhaps this woman is on her way home to see a family she doesn't like, just like Ms. Radant. Ahh, that explains the bad attitude.

Twenty minutes before scheduled departure, and we are all invited to line up for boarding . . . all of us. No organized groupings or sections, we all just mad-dash it toward the door. I don't take this as a good sign, for it usually means the plane is less than tiny.

I am correct. At the end of the boarding ramp a bus is waiting, rather than a plane. We will now be bussed to our plane. Cranky Lady just put the driver in a headlock and is threatening to "really lose it" if he doesn't go faster. It is going to be a good flight. I move on to a story by Jay McInerney about the tradition of angry outbursts that has become a staple at his testosterone-laden Thanksgiving table. It's a family of brothers, one of whom is a writer who wrote his greatest works based on the family's torment . . . and eventually got the crap beaten out of him when his brothers got fed up with having their family slandered by his "creative license." Note to self, don't write about your family.

I finally get on the actual plane and walk down the aisle praying to the travel gods that my seat buddy won't be sick, or creepy, or talkative. As I approach I see an unassuming blonde, already fast asleep. Score . . . it is a holiday travel miracle! And then the gentleman who will be sitting across the aisle from me finds his seat. I use the term gentleman loosely . . . he is actually the tallest, broadest, most enormous human being I have ever seen in my life. As he attempts to origami himself into a shape that will fit into the seat, I cower in fear that a stray hand might accidentally swing around and decapitate me. He finally gets himself situated; one leg stretched all the way down the aisle to where Cranky Lady is complaining four rows ahead. He quickly falls asleep, but twitches in his dreams, and every time he has one of these twitches I impulsively throw my book in front of my face to fend off a potential blow to the jaw. By this point I am deep into a story by Daniel Blythe about all of the potential dangers that surround simple holiday traditions, from poisonous foliage to kitchen mishaps. I think death by fellow air travelers should be added to this list.

I land in Cincinnati, and simultaneously finish *The Dreaded Feast*, closing out the whole epic adventure through travel and literature with the beloved words of David Sedaris. I have now been awake for twenty-four hours. I don't remember what day it is, what I was doing a few hours ago, or even what I had intended to write when I began back at LaGuardia. This entry has traveled just as many miles and mishaps as I have. Within minutes of stepping off the plane, though, I already see an old friend who happened to be flying in at the same time. And I emerge from the gates to the eager face of my mother, waiting anxiously to wrap me in her tiny little arms for an extra-long hug. On the drive home I round the bend to see the beautiful sight of my city skyline . . . and by city, I mean Cincinnati. My dogs attack me when I walk in the front door of my childhood home, and my little brother—bearded and smelling of patchouli—greets me with a headlock and an immediate playful quip. I am home.

Lesson #13:
Get Over Yourself

Going home for Thanksgiving did not appease my homesickness at all. In fact, it made things worse. As I climbed in the cab from LaGuardia and instructed the driver to take me back to my dingy digs in Brooklyn, I felt like I was being kidnapped, dragged somewhere against my will. I was the kidnapper, though. I was also just overly dramatic and self-pitying . . . and talking to myself once again:

Self-Pitying Julia: Sigh . . . Why me? Why does everything go wrong for me? I hate my job, I miss my family and friends, and I can't even figure out what I'm supposed to be pursuing. Why can't I just get paid to do what I love? What do I love? Why doesn't anyone love me? Why am I always so alone? I am a hostage in my own life! My soul is slowly dying! My talent is slipping away! And I'm turning another year older in a few days . . . ohhhh where is the time going?! I'm wasting my life away and . . .

Tough-Love Julia: DEAR GOD SHUT UP.

Self-Pitying Julia: (whimpering) Wha . . . what? Why are you so mean? Why is everything so mean in this cruel, cruel . . .

Tough-Love Julia: OH MY GOD SERIOUSLY. Seriously. Do you have a roof over your head at night?

Self-Pitying Julia: Well . . . yes, but it's not very . . .

Tough-Love Julia: Yes. Yes you do. Do you have food in the cabinets?

Self-Pitying Julia: Not right now because I need to go grocery shopping! It's HARD to lug all those groceries home on the train and . . .

Tough-Love Julia: Oh shut up and just do it. Do you have money to buy those groceries? Yes. Do you have money in the bank? Yes. More than enough. Did you not just spend $100 on a new pair of stiletto boots?

Self-Pitying Julia: Yes, but those were an early birthday present to myself! Plus, money doesn't buy you happiness . . .

Tough-Love Julia: Cut the shit. You are fine. You are going to be fine. You may not be happy now, but you will be happy again. You are safe, and warm, and taken care of. You have people who love you. And you are turning twenty-three, not seventy-three. Get over yourself. Your problems are not real problems. They are just challenges.

Silence.

Sometimes you just have to smack yourself in the face.

Journal Entry,
December 7, 2009

All My Lovin'

Two things happened to me within the past few days that have brought me incredible happiness (albeit, nostalgia) and wisdom:

1: I celebrated my twenty-third birthday.

2: I decorated for Christmas.

Birthdays have always been something magical for me. At times it was troubling because I would build up such expectations for surprise and wonderment that they could not be met . . . and the only thing worse than being disappointed is being disappointed on your birthday.

As the years have come and gone I've gotten better at entering into the days preceding my birthday with Zen-like stealth. I've realized that all I ever really want is to have all the people I love around me. This year I set my sights REALLY low. I am far, far away from so very many people that I love dearly. I am in a brand new city (and a tough one, at

that). And I think I am going through what John Mayer re-
ferred to as a "quarter-life crisis."

One minute after midnight, December 4. Phone call comes
in from my former roommates, my eternal soul sisters, two of
my loveliest lady friends. They want to be the first to wish me
a happy birthday.

I immediately burst into tears.

Ten after midnight, December 4. NYC roommate/partner in
crime peeks in to check on my sobbing. Understands without
asking that I simply need to cry. Wishes me a happy birthday.

The next morning I walk into the kitchen where home-
made granola is sitting, waiting for me, from said roommate.
More tears. Blessed tears, though.

Throughout the course of the rest of the day I received
more love from people near and far than I even knew what to
do with. I talked to all the right people, got messages and
emails from all the right people, cards handmade from the kids
I take care of . . . it was a birthday miracle, to say the least.

As I climbed into bed in the wee hours of the morning on
December 5, after a long night of celebration, dancing, drink-
ing, and good ol' late-night café eating with some dear old
pals—I paused in utter humility and gratitude to the Universe.
I do not exactly know how I came to be blessed with SO
many incredible people. People that made a point to let me
know that near or far, they were thinking about me. I love
these people, because they reminded me on this day (not un-
like any other day, but special still) that I am loved and worthy of love. They reminded me that I am blessed, and worthy
of blessings. They reminded me that I am SO far from being
alone. So very far from loneliness because I am most certainly
being taken care of, not only by this marvelous Universe and
its Creator, but by a world of people in it. I am humbled by

how blessed I felt on my twenty-third birthday . . . and I hope it is a feeling that I will not soon forget.

So then today I decorated for Christmas: went to Target; bought a fake tree; went WILD in the holiday section; came home with way too much stuff; went to town on the apartment.

I was listening to *Christmas with the Rat Pack* (the only holiday album worth listening to, in my opinion) and "Have Yourself a Merry Little Christmas" came on. I love how age makes you understand music and lyrics so much more. For a million reasons, the song made more sense to me now than it ever has before.

In listening, I realized that as life moves on, your heart gets spread thinner and thinner across the miles and years. My love is scattered across this country. And the chances of me ever having all of the people I love with me at once is slim to none, and it will get even slimmer with each passing day. I will never have a Thanksgiving, a birthday, or a Christmas where I am not blessed to have so much love in my life, but at the same time saddened to be away from some of these special people.

All of this is to say, that the celebration of my twenty-third year of being alive, in conjunction with the decorating for my first NY Christmas, has led me to believe that all we really have to gain from this life is the people we love and the memories we create. I think when we live with this pursuit, other wonderful by-products come . . . but we have to start with the people. On my birthday I wasn't nostalgic for the plays I had been in or directed, or the acclaim I had gotten from any previous work. I was thankful for the people in my life.

So there you go. Go hug someone. Go tell them you love them. Send out a prayer of gratitude for the love you have given and received. Listen to some *Christmas with the Rat Pack*. And contemplate your priorities.

Lesson #14:
When All Else Fails, Dance

My birthday set into motion a month of pure celebration. I spent December enjoying life and the people in it; forgetting the rest. I forced a smile onto my face each morning before heading in to take care of the kids . . . and it helped. I became a social director of sorts: organizing nights out and dinners and game nights; excuses for people to simply get together and laugh. I walked through the open-air holiday markets that filled the city, and soaked up the spirit of the season, feeling grateful that I could spend a little extra this year on nice gifts for the people I loved. I let the lovely things take over my mind and chose to spend a month worry free. My quarter-life crisis would just have to wait until after the New Year; this month was for me to enjoy.

I remember so distinctly one special night at the end of December, just a couple days before I was heading back to Cincinnati for Christmas. I had gathered a few of my friends to listen to The Musicians as they played one of their gigs at a little pub that had become a sanctuary of sorts over the past few months. Holiday lights illuminated Bleecker Street that night, Christmas trees twinkled in the corners and a few snowflakes fluttered down from the night sky. As the night went on, our group grew, friends new and old joined the party, and before we knew it everyone was dancing. We danced for hours. I will never forget the split second when I paused to catch my breath and I just looked around at the people who surrounded me. Everyone looked so full of joy, not a single worry on anyone's face. These were my people. This was mine to enjoy and appreciate. I took a mental picture. I wanted to remember this snapshot. It was the kind of moment in time that you would look back on years later and realize how lucky you truly had been in your life. Whether I could appreciate it fully then or not, I knew one day I would. Tomorrow would bring plenty of time to worry; that night, I was going to dance. I was going to celebrate all the small victories: I had made it to NYC and I had created new friendships. I had simply woken up every morning for four months and made it through the days, both good and bad. I had kept moving, I had kept breathing, and I had continued to believe. Small victories, people. Small victories.

Journal Entry,
December 19, 2009

It Is The Indescribable

I am wary sometimes of showing people how much love I have brewing amongst these little bones of mine. I can have my down days like the rest, and I can throw out sarcasm with a one-two punch. Most of the time, though, I just love. I do the giddy dance a lot, when I'm alone, to show my gratitude for people, places, and things.

Mostly people and places. Friends often tease me for how I tend to zone out sometimes, especially in social settings. I am not actually zoning out, I am willing myself to remember all of the details of the moment. I like gathering people around me, and then just watching them be happy. I like seeing nights carry on with such joy, and no one realizing how happy they look and feel.

I have sappily filled this book with words of gratitude, but I can never seem to sufficiently say how blessed I truly feel. Life got harder for me when I moved to NY. Things got harder. Emotions became more real. Time became daunting. But it seems as if all of that difficult terrain brought me to a

place where I can look at the life I've lead so far, and the possibilities before me, and simply stand in awe of what I've been
blessed with. Mostly, it is the people. I don't think I've ever
appreciated all of the wonderful, stellar, talented, beautiful,
kind, and loving people in my life as much as I have come to
recently. And just as soon as I think I've met all of the best
people this world has to offer, I meet someone new and
equally phenomenal. It is more than I know what to do with
sometimes . . . so I write . . . and yet I can never get the words
perfectly right.

It is the indescribable. The love I have is beyond words.

I hope you are blessed with such love for everything. Or I
hope you find the pursuit of such love most noble. And I hope
you would devote your life to this kind of power, if nothing
else. I can tell you, it may be beyond words, but it adds a
sparkle to even the most mundane of days.

Lesson #15: Just Decide

"May your coming year be filled with magic and dreams and good madness. I hope you read some fine books and kiss someone who thinks you're wonderful, and don't forget to make some art—write or draw or build or sing or live as only you can. And I hope, somewhere in the next year, you surprise yourself."

–NEIL GAIMAN

Every New Year I have certain rituals; the "It's My Year!" rituals. Doesn't everyone say this? With each passing December 31 we say that this will be the year when everything goes right. Things that are going well will get a million times better and things that are going awfully will magically change. We will fall in love, we will make our fortunes doing what we love, and we will accomplish all our dreams and be infinitely happy every single day. So often, though, it's a horoscope-like wish. We tell ourselves that all of these things will simply fly toward us. We aren't really willing ourselves forward to capture the things we desire, it's more of a desperate plea to God and the Universe: "Please, *please*, let this year be the year."

If ever I needed a new year to be better than the last, it was this one. Yes, I had been telling myself repeatedly, "you were blessed this past year, you were so very blessed." The self-encouragement was wearing thin, though. Remember, quarter-life crisis had started to creep up on me back in November and December, and I had simply said "Not today, sir. Come back later."

Quarter-Life Crisis: I'M BAAAAAAAACK!!

Julia: Ugh. Go away. I don't want what you're selling.

Quarter-Life Crisis: Ok, well I'm just going to leave it here by your bed where you can trip over it every morning. Here in this nice little gift basket we have some Self-Doubt, Insecurity, Confusion, and a couple of nice little pamphlets entitled "Why Your Friends Are More Successful Than You" and "Reasons Why You May End Up A Failure." Enjoy!

Julia: No stop . . . wait, TAKE IT WITH YOU! I DON'T WANT IT. Do you see this room? I don't have space for any more clutter.

Quarter-Life Crisis: Oooh sorry, it's out of my hands now. Ok, well . . . BYE!

I tripped over my little gift basket every single morning for weeks. I tried throwing a blanket over it, but I tripped on it nonetheless. I tried shoving it in a corner, but sneaky little bugger would still find a way to trip me up. I would have shoved it under the bed, but I was still sleeping on the air mattress so I was out of luck.

One evening after leaving a particularly challenging day of work, shins bleeding from all the tumbles I had taken over my little quarter-life crisis, I sat in a Starbucks near Thirty-fourth Street and shamelessly sobbed to a new friend that I had gained in the city. I hated who I had become. I hated the unhappiness that was winning over my optimism. I hated that I was the friend who always needed to be encouraged, rather than the friend that was doing the encouraging. I was not me; I felt like a shell of someone I had once known. I cried and cried while she calmly listened, and ended my saga with the utterance of my darkest and most deeply rooted fear: that this would never end. I hadn't admitted to anyone yet that what caused me the most anguish was this fear that I would never feel better . . . that life would always be like this, that I would always feel this unhappy.

My friend waited until I had finished and took a pause. Then, she simply looked me dead in the eye and said, "Well, you have to keep going anyway. You still have to wake up every day and you still have to put one foot in front of the other. You just have to do it, and keep doing it. Things will change, but maybe you need a little more patience. A plane takes off against the wind, after all."

As I sat stunned and processing, and she excused herself to go to the restroom, I stared out the window at a nearly perfect full moon. A whisper passed through me that said, "You, too, will once again be full and whole like this moon. That is the journey you are on. It is a journey though, you can either commit to it or not. Just decide."

So in that moment, in that Starbucks with mascara running down my face, I decided. I decided I would take on the challenge to keep moving through my own fears and insecurities until I felt whole and confident again. Maybe this year wouldn't be the year where everything went right, but it would be the year where I dug in and persisted in spite of anything that came at me. A whole new journey began that night.

Journal Entry,
January 30, 2010

A Quote

"I would rather be ash than dust! I would rather that my spark should burn out in a brilliant blaze than it should be stifled by dry rot. I would rather be a superb meteor, every atom of me in magnificent glow, than a sleepy and permanent planet. The proper function of man is to live, not to exist. I shall not waste my days trying to prolong them. I shall use my time."

                                        −JACK LONDON

Lesson #16:
Get Busy Living

Over the next couple of months I was in the business of being busy. I took on a volunteer job just to get me out of the snake pit of my own mind. I covered as many events as I could for the magazine, spitting out two or three articles a week. I stayed out late with friends dancing and enjoying music. I started meeting with various artists, dreaming up various projects, or maybe just dreaming. I ran here, there, and everywhere, if only to avoid being alone with my own thoughts.

Somewhere in there I felt my body revolting, but I didn't have time to be slowed down. Sleep was for the weak. I was a warrior on this new journey back to happiness. I wasn't actually making myself any happier, but I was certainly not leaving any free moments in the day to think about whether I was or was not. If I could just keep moving, I thought, everything would be ok.

In March I took a week and went to visit friends in Chicago. The minute I arrived I crashed, having slowed down for the first time in nearly three months. I felt so much more at home on my friend's couch than I did in my own "home" back in Brooklyn . . . but that was fine, I said. Crash here, recharge the batteries, and then fly back to New York ready for battle again.

When I woke up my first morning back in NYC, I begrudged having to go back to nanny land. I felt more tired after my week away than I had before I left. I also had the most enormous zit over my eyebrow . . . just appallingly large. Perfect. I smothered my face in makeup until I just gave up and headed into the battle zone again. I was run down, I could tell, and my head pounded, but I couldn't afford to sit still. If I stopped moving, in this city especially, all of the horrible self-doubts that I had would come flooding back. No stopping. Just keep moving, I told myself. Whatever you have to do, just do not stop.

That night I was scheduled to do a special event and interview. It was the biggest thing I'd hooked since being in New York: I was supposed to interview Sheryl Crow on the red carpet.

All day I dreaded it. Sounds crazy, but I was terrified. What the hell was I going to ask Sheryl Crow? I didn't know how to operate these red carpet events. I didn't have a plus-one to take, and I didn't feel well. It was something new and uncertain and I simply didn't want to do it. I felt like taking a page out of girl-child's book and throwing myself on the floor, fists pounding and screaming, "I DON'T WANNA!"

Leaving work I did approximately ten false starts for home. I would decide I wasn't going to go to the event and head for home. Then I would stop myself short of getting on the train to Brooklyn and buck myself up to head toward the theatre. Then I would turn back toward home. Then back toward Sheryl. Home. Sheryl. Home. Sheryl.

You are going to regret not doing this more than you'll regret doing it.

FINE. I went. I can honestly say it was exhilarating. Not the event itself, not even the interview, but simply the doing. I could now say that I was the kind of person who did the things she was most afraid of. I was not one to shrink back. Always do what you are afraid to do; for the knowledge that you are the kind of person who will fight their own fear. "Fear is the thief of dreams," someone once said. That night I understood better what that meant; it was another small victory for me. Julia: 1; NYC: 0.

Lesson #17:
Some Things Can't Be Outrun

I woke up the next morning and my eye was swollen shut. Fantastic. Just freaking fantastic. I stared at my Quasimodo-esque face in the mirror and started laughing like a crazy person, which bled into crying, which led to me laughing even harder. Twelve hours ago I had been interviewing Sheryl Crow and now my face was an excruciatingly painful disaster. I stared at my swollen, disfigured face, and began to think that this zit was maybe not a zit at all. As I desperately called around to find the best walk-in clinic, and heard the water start to plink in the pot by my bed as it fell from my ceiling, I had to stop and just really appreciate this moment. This was what we call a "low point." I hoped that this was my low point, because that meant that I would get to climb back up.

My theory of that moment being my low point was confirmed later when the doctor diagnosed me with shingles. What is shingles, you ask? Shingles is like chicken pox for adults, only not as fun. What's that you say? Chicken pox *isn't* fun? Exactly. Shingles is even *less* fun. It is incredibly painful and horrifyingly ugly. The right side of my face was now temporarily paralyzed, with ugly blisters climbing down my

eyebrow. To add insult to injury, they put you on herpes med-
ication to clear it up. And because I was so young, the first
thing they wanted to check for at the clinic was HIV.

So yes, this was my low point: scheduling an HIV test,
knowing full well that it was entirely impossible for me to
have HIV, and filling a prescription for Valtrex while the little
old lady pharmacist gave me the stink eye.

Shingles also meant that I had to pretty much go on bed
rest for about two weeks. No working, no going out, no nothing. All day, every day, in bed, alone. So much for not being
alone with my own mind. I was about to have over three hun-
dred hours alone with my own mind.

It was the most discouraged I could remember myself ever
having been. The entire month of March, in fact, felt like the
deepest pit I'd been in. It wasn't the circumstance that felt the
most defeating, but the fact that I found myself believing that
things might never get better. There was this overwhelming
sadness that I awoke with every single day, and I started to believe that it would never go away. How could I assume that
things would get better, when for the past six months they had
gotten increasingly worse and more confusing? How do you
muster up the proof in your life that things will change when
the only evidence you have is suggesting otherwise?

For two weeks I spent all day, every day, in bed. In the beginning I watched bad TV online and clicked through albums
of photographs from times when I had been happy and fulfilled. I watched all six seasons of *Lost*, from beginning to
end . . . only to be disgusted with the sheer volume of wasted
time that was. I wallowed in my own self-pity, taking phone
calls from concerned friends and not even attempting to put my
usual positive spin on the situation. One day I decided to take
a walk through the park by my apartment, if only to get out of

my pathetic cave. As I walked, mulling over the thoughts and feelings that I'd been running from for two months, I began to get more and more worked up. I was sad, angry, resentful . . . appalled. I was appalled at my situation. I was appalled that my story was playing out like this, so far from what I'd ever imagined and hoped for myself. As that anger rose I stopped in the middle of the park, totally alone, and without even thinking I started yelling at the God that I believed had brought me here and left me defenseless. "You did this!" I screamed. "You got me here, so what now? What are you going to do now?" I threw my hands wide and said "I cannot stay like this! I cannot survive like this. I am not meant to be this unhappy! *SOMETHING* has to change! It *MUST* change!"

And then I was silent. The wind blew a little around me. I was staring straight up into the cloudy sky, and as I exhaled I let my gaze settle across the vastness of the park. I found myself staring at a huge and expansive tree that was planted right in the center of the big, open field and it made me feel calm, for no particular reason that I could understand. In that moment I felt an answer start to rise in me; the whispers of a God who fought back with gentleness, perhaps. Or maybe it was my own strength and inner being breaking through the false beliefs that were stacked like bricks on my spirit.

Yes. It does have to change. It must change, therefore it will change.

That was my answer. That was all I needed and, truthfully, all I could handle. Things had to change. Non-negotiable. So they would. I didn't know how; I didn't know what I would have to do to make the change. In that moment, though, all I needed was a deeply rooted, gut-pulsating sense that change would come . . . because it had to. I was capable of nothing more than just clinging desperately to one simple fact: things would change.

Journal Entry,
April 21, 2010

I Forget What I Want To Be . . . When I Grow Up

Lesson #18:
Belief Is A Powerful Thing

April began a thirty-day countdown toward something that I'd been looking forward to for months: I was going home in so many senses of the word. Not only would I be returning to my family and old friends in Cincinnati for a couple of days, but I was also going back my other home. I was going back to the first home I'd created on my own: Ann Arbor. I was going back to the apartment I'd lived in for three years, to do a show with the greatest artistic family I'd ever known.

That silly little Potter play that I'd mentioned before, the one that had led to the birth of a company called StarKid Productions? Well, that little play was about to get a big brother. Though we were spread all over the country and had not been together for almost a year, we had made a commitment to return to Ann Arbor, to the little studio theatre that had been our playground for years. For two weeks we would return to a prior life and do what we knew how to do best: work, laugh, and screw around . . . and hope that we ended up with a play.

One night, about a week before I was set to leave for this two-week adventure, I professed a secret hope to a group of new friends I'd met: "This trip. This play . . . it is going to change my life. It *has* to change my life."

I didn't profess it because I actually believed it, but because I *needed* to believe it. Even if it was a false belief, even if I was just bullshitting myself . . . I needed a belief and that was the one I chose. Belief is a funny thing. We need it desperately but rarely trust it entirely. Belief asks that you decide to put merit in things unseen. It asks that you commit to something that may not prove itself in return. I was realizing that when you don't have an answer, when you feel like you don't have much of anything, even just a belief is enough to get you through. The promise of its fulfillment is secondary.

And so I had to believe: "These two weeks will change my life."

Journal Entry,
May 1, 2010

When I Get There

Airports are so exciting. I feel like a kid every time I am preparing to fly somewhere, if only for the anticipation of the airports.

Right now I'm sitting in LaGuardia, waiting to fly back home to Cincinnati for a short visit before driving up to my second home, Ann Arbor, for some pure and crazy madness—Camp Hogwarts; two weeks with some of my closest friends and creative soul mates, creating a sequel to that silly and wonderful Potter play we did one whole year ago.

Marc Broussard is playing in my ear, and I'm thinking about how much has happened in a year, and how none of it was what I expected it to be. Sometimes better, sometimes worse, but always surprising.

I'm also thinking a lot about homes and what makes a home, and how I ache for the Midwest most days, but still something whispers in my ear, "New York is where you are supposed to be."

I'm wondering if I've enjoyed and appreciated the journey of this past year as much as I could have. There is a delicious ambiguity that is just not always given grace.

I feel the distance a lot, but especially when I travel back. Tonight it will take me a car, a bus, and an airplane just to get me back to where I began—and after all that travel and effort I always start to wonder if it's worth it; to be so far from everything I know and love in pursuit of something yet unseen. I think one day I will say yes, but for now it's still a question mark on my life.

What I do know for certain is that the next two weeks may quite possibly give me some of the greatest memories of my life. And in spite of all my worries and anxieties, I'm the luckiest because I have an abundance of lovely people who I yearn to get back to—and starting today I get to go back.

And we will laugh and trade stories and catch each other up on our varied and separate lives. And these people, both my biological family and my creative family, they probably don't know most of the time how they keep me going, even though my life may be a mess.

Home. I get to go home. A return to roots, so that I can remember how to grow.

It's a big life, but a small world . . . and you just never know what's coming for you.

Lesson #19: You'll Know It When You See It

I walked into the studio on the first day of rehearsal and I felt so immediately and inexplicably at home that it took my breath away. The happiest faces in the world surrounded me. I stared at these people, many of whom I'd known for several years, and they stood both familiar and mysterious to me. There was a sense of comfortable invitation for us to unravel even more exciting tidbits about one another. Where have you been? What have you been doing? What has life taught you, that I haven't been a part of, over these past fleeting months?

In the first hours of our first rehearsal, something broke open in me. Laughter took over me that was stronger than any laugh I'd had in a while. It was as if this thing, this ball of *something* that had settled in my gut over time, was suddenly set loose; energy, excitement, and joy flying through my system. It was a familiar feeling because it was the feeling I had come to know as my own happiness. A mere month ago I had been convinced that I might never know that feeling again, that perhaps it was silly child's play to feel that free. That feeling had returned, though. Aha! This is the stuff of life! To feel free, joyful, excited, and inspired. This was the stuff that had shaped me and guided me thus far. This was the stuff. If I'd lost it but found it again, then I knew it must be right. Child's play? Perhaps. Well then, I would live life like a child. For God's sake, I'd throw myself on the ground in a full-blown tantrum if that was the fight it was going to take to get my happiness and get it for good.

I grasped at every hour that passed with desperate possessiveness. There was a running tally in my head of how many minutes, hours, days had passed, and how many I had left. We had taken over our old theatre building and it became a factory for us: in one room choreography was taught, in another, scenes were blocked. At one point a piano got pushed out onto the courtyard so that music could be rehearsed while soaking up a little sun. It was perfect, at least to me it was. We were running around on broomsticks and choreographing dance numbers and I just wanted to yell, "How amazing is this?! How are we all not jumping with joy that these are our days?!"

There was one thing that I couldn't help but say to everyone, over and over again: "We should be doing this. All of the time. We could do this for real, and we should. This should be our life."

Journal Entry,
June 4, 2010

Some Things Are So Good They Must Be Told

"Desiderata" by Max Ehrman
Go placidly amidst the noise and haste, and remember what peace there may be in silence. As far as possible without surrender be on good terms with all persons. Speak your truth quietly and clearly; and listen to others, even to the dull and the ignorant; they too have their story.

Avoid loud and aggressive persons; they are vexatious to the spirit. If you compare yourself with others, you may become vain or bitter; for always there will be greater and lesser persons than yourself.

Enjoy your achievements as well as your plans. Keep interested in your own career, however humble; it is a real possession in the changing fortunes of time.

Exercise caution in your business affairs; for the world is full of trickery. But let this not blind you to what virtue there is; many persons strive for high ideals, and everywhere life is full of heroism.

Be yourself. Especially, do not feign affection. Neither be cynical about love; for in the face of all aridity and disenchantment it is as perennial as the grass.

Take kindly the counsel of the years, gracefully surrendering the things of youth. Nurture strength of spirit to shield you in sudden misfortune. But do not distress yourself with dark imaginings. Many fears are born of fatigue and loneliness.

Beyond a wholesome discipline, be gentle with yourself. You are a child of the universe, no less than the trees and the stars; you have a right to be here.

And whether or not it is clear to you, no doubt the universe is unfolding as it should. Therefore be at peace with God, whatever you conceive Him to be, and whatever your labours and aspirations, in the noisy confusion of life keep peace with your soul. With all its shams, drudgery, and broken dreams, it is still a beautiful world. Be cheerful.

Strive to be happy.

Lesson #20: You'll See It When You Know It

"Do not let your fire go out, spark by irreplaceable spark in the hopeless swaps of the not-quite, the not-yet, and the not-at-all. Do not let the hero in your soul perish in lonely frustration for the life you deserved and have never been able to reach. The world you desire can be won. It exists . . . it is real . . . it is possible . . . it's yours."

–AYN RAND

Those few weeks back in the Midwest had flown by far too quickly. Before I knew it I was sobbing into my Caribou Coffee in a flickering, dingy terminal of the Detroit airport. I was sad to leave my friends, sad to leave the magic of those couple of weeks, but also sad in a new way. Sad because this time, on this return to NYC, I knew I had to make a plan and make a change. "Enough is enough," my friends had said with their tough love. No more excuses; get busy making life work for you. Not busy in the way I'd been running from my own mind in the prior months, but busy believing that this was the beginning of the best that was yet to come. This was not actually sad at all, it was empowering, but also meant "busting butt" was going to take on a whole new connotation.

The question became, "What do you want? *What do you want?*" It whispered me to sleep at night. It replaced the sun

99

that didn't reach through the windows of my apartment. It drowned out the screaming of cranky children and swallowed up any pain or loneliness that I was feeling. "What do you want?" became the most freeing thing in my world. In my heart I knew exactly what I wanted; I wanted to be surrounded by the people I loved, the people who inspired me. I wanted to be working in an artistic family. I wanted to sustain myself on the work that I was meant to do, and I wanted to be challenged in that work daily. All of that seemed a little demanding though, for my bruised and beaten self-esteem, so I said, "Anything else but what I'm doing now, please!"

I flung myself into applying for any and all jobs that were not my current one. I replied to every craigslist ad that anyone posted in the entire New York area. I asked friends of friends of friends of friends if they had any leads. I went on interviews, took internships, and pursued. I remembered something I'd been told once when I was younger: sometimes you just have to move, take action, and just go. When you show that willingness to go for it, God and the Universe will meet you there and do you one better.

In the first week of June, on a clear summer's night when the moon was very full and there were more than the usual number of stars in the sky, a phone call came in. The voice on the other end delivered a message, an invitation, really, that altered everything: move to Chicago. Together. We're going to do this together. It won't be easy, but it will be worth it. Move to Chicago—let's start a revolution.

The most immediate *yes* of my life came leaping out of me. No second thoughts, no turning back. A terrifying idea, it made no sense at all, and yet all the sense in the world. Yes means yes, and when your gut says yes, you'd better follow through.

Yes, I will move to Chicago. Yes, I will take this adventure with you. *Yes*.

Journal Entry,
July 26, 2010

Life Is Happening

"Let life happen to you. Believe me: life is in the right, always."

–RAINER MARIA RILKE

Well life is certainly happening. Lots of changes, lots of excitement, ups and downs, surprises, laughter, tears, love, and confusion. Life is certainly happening.

It was about one year ago that I started this record of the adventures to come. That year marker seemed so far off at the time. Now here I stand, slightly beaten, but surely stronger, and pointed in a new direction. New York and I had a tumultuous time together, but I've always been good at walking away from my relationships at the right time, with the right appreciation for what was good and necessary—with an understanding of why it was important to move through that season.

Once upon a time, when I was much younger, I picked up a book about a boy named Harry Potter and I fell in love with him and his story . . . and I followed those stories all the way through to the end, and I cried when I closed the final page. Little did I know that one day that boy and those stories would change the course of my life entirely.

Once upon a time, a little over a year ago, I showed up on a Sunday to paint some set pieces and help out some friends who were preparing to put on a silly musical about that charming Potter boy. Little did I know that being in the right place at the right time on that Sunday would set into motion a sequence of events that led me to this particular moment in time, where Fate has stepped in and placed a new adventure and journey ahead of me with a lovely group of people known as StarKids.

Life certainly happens. I think it is a fight every day to get out of your own way and allow it, but it is when I allow myself to die to my own dreams, and relax into the confusion and uncertainty of life, that my truest dreams and desires have actually taken shape right before my eyes.

And then . . . you jump. You lunge and leap into the outline of the life you begged for; you fill in the blanks on your way down. That moment of peace before the Great Fall. That instant of stillness right before your heart starts pumping stronger and faster, and you know the time is now, no turning back.

A new chapter is beginning, and I want to cherish every moment of this next coming year. One day the winds will slow, and the storm will calm, and I'll want to remember every second of the insanity that is about to commence.

Let the games begin.

Lesson #21: Know Thyself

At the end of August (just five days short of my one-year anniversary with New York City) I sold my furniture, dropped my air conditioner out of the window, packed my bags, and loaded up a rental car with the haphazard scraps of my life. I said tearful goodbyes to the countless friends I hadn't even realized I'd made in my difficult year, and with what I hope was some grace and gratitude, I said farewell to the city that had broken me down so that I might know the real stuff that I was made of. With my brother in the seat next to me, I cursed my way through Chinatown, crawled in traffic through the Lincoln Tunnel, and then . . . I was free.

As I drove on open roads heading toward the truest home I'd ever known, I watched the sunset and let tears fall down my cheeks as one of those now-familiar whispers came through me:

Now can you see your own strength? What you can go through, and come out of in one piece? You will never be forgotten; you will never be left behind. You were born with a warrior's heart.

There are countless things in this world worse than what I've experienced. In fact I have been abundantly blessed, and I know that my pains are minimal in comparison to those of so many worse off than I. Yet, a rough year is a rough year, a rough time is a rough time, no matter the circumstances. Having known your own happiness and fulfillment and then lost it is a hardship; a death of its own kind. The journey back is the important part. The journey itself is important.

I was born with a warrior's heart. I know that now. From the time I was young I talked back too much, dreamed dreams that were too big, and spoke too boldly for most people's liking. The world wants to squelch such enthusiasm; the mundanity of life will fight to smother the fires within. I, though, was not born of those who shrink back. I am more than a conqueror, and so are you.

We are all born with the heart of a champion . . . it's the only thing that makes sense. Generations before us have lived lives of passion so that we might be empowered to do greater things than they could ever dream. Your calling might not be glamorous, your mission might be singular and uneasy, but you were meant to be great in your own way. Your happiness is your greatness; your giving to the lives around you is your greatness. Your commitment to making this life better than the cynics say it can be—that is your greatness.

I know now that I was born with a warrior's heart—a heart that does not accept a muted, mechanized form of life. I was born with a heart that told me beauty was important, and love paramount. This heart screams against the dull pain of simply existing. This heart demands the best, and it will fight its way out of my ribcage to pursue that.

This warrior's heart of mine may upset some, it may offend others, it may even scare me at times. But this heart is the greatest gift I have. It leads me through battles and it pioneers new planes. Above all else, it always leads me back to where I am supposed to be.

Thus, I learned to know myself and know my heart. I am young still, and I'm sure I have many journeys ahead. This journey, though, showed me the truest truth I might ever know: I was born with a warrior's heart. I am not one to shrink back. Though the adventures and challenges to come are many, the best is yet to come.

"I took a deep breath and listened to the old bray of my heart: I am, I am, I am."

—SYLVIA PLATH

SPECIAL THANKS

To my parents, once again, for their unconditional love and support. Aaron and Lauren, my partners in crime . . . you were the best part of my time in NYC. Martin and Craig, for being a musical lifeboat. C3 Manhattan, and the family I made there, for empowering me, and giving reason to my journey. To all of my unbelievable friends near and far, for making this life so full and blessed. My brother Mark, for letting me use his incredible image for my cover art. My sister Anna for simply being cute. And to the audience that has given me a platform for my thoughts and words. I am the luckiest.

Made in the USA
Middletown, DE
23 November 2015